Pastimes

A comedy

Brian Jeffries

Samuel French — London
New York - Toronto - Hollywood

Please see page iv for further copyright information.

PASTIMES

First presented at The Mill at Sonning on 22nd October 1996 with the following cast:

Sam	Roy Heather
Connie	Patricia Kane
Bill	Barry Gosney
Winifred	Geraldine Newman
Linda	Julie Burnage

Directed by Sally Hughes
Designed by Jacqueline Hutson
Lighting by Roslyn Nash

Subsequently toured by Millett Productions Ltd, commencing at the Theatre Royal, Nottingham on 26th January 1998, with the following cast:

Sam	William Gaunt
Connie	Rosemary Leach
Bill	Barry Gosney
Winifred	Geraldine Newman
Linda	Keely Gainey

Directed by Sally Hughes
Designed by Roy D Bell
Lighting by Roger Frith

COPYRIGHT INFORMATION

(See also page ii)

CHARACTERS

Sam, early sixties
Bill, early sixties
Connie, early sixties
Winifred, early sixties
Linda, 17

The action of the play takes place in the kitchen and living-room of a small café in a seaside town

Time: Late summer. The present

SYNOPSIS OF SCENES

NOTE

The café serves light meals and snacks and is normally well run by Sam and Bill, with efficiency, care and cleanliness.

Apart from preparing the meals, there are tasks to be carried out continually in the kitchen: tidying up, washing up, wiping up, keeping kettles topped up and close to boiling, washing hands, wiping surfaces, replenishing pre-prepared items … etc.

Brian Jeffries

ACT I
SCENE 1

The kitchen and living-room of a small café in a seaside town. An evening in late summer

The set is split: to one side is the kitchen of the café, to the other a living-room, with a door connecting the two

The kitchen is well-equipped, clean and orderly. In the US wall is a swinging door and a smoked glass window, beyond which is the unseen café. Among the equipment are: a stainless steel sink and drainer, modern cooker, microwave oven, cool chest, purpose built shelves (for crockery), refrigerator, freezer and a small hand washbasin. There are kitchen units with working surfaces (not modern); one surface has a notebook on it. On one wall there is a small varnished board with seven numbered hooks; hooks one, two, three, four and six have orders hanging from them. On a shelf there is a small tape recorder which transmits classical music to the café

The living-room is plain. There is a window in the US wall, and a door which leads to the street. There is an open planked wooden staircase, a carpet-sweeper propped beneath it. A small dining table and four small chairs, a small armchair and a large drinks cabinet or sideboard are the main items of furniture. There is also a small table on which is an unfinished game of Ludo, and another which holds the telephone. Some basic wall shelving holds a large number of paperback books

The CURTAIN *rises. Bill is working in the kitchen. His actions are unhurried and precise*

Sam enters from the café

Sam Table three: two coffees, two blackcurrant cheesecake.
Bill Two coffees it is. (*He begins preparing the coffees*)
Sam The young girl is still there.
Bill Table six?
Sam Yes. And the four noisy people on table five have left prematurely. They were the egg and chip brigade. (*He mimics them*) "What, no chips, guv?" I've sent them packing.

Bill The usual quip?

Sam Of course. "This is not the place if you want chips."

Bill Did they laugh?

Sam No — chip lovers rarely laugh. (*He prepares the cheesecake during the following*) I'm thinking table three are from Suffolk. Not a strong dialect. But I'll mark it down. (*He makes a note in his book*)

Bill Really. Are you confident?

Sam Very.

Bill I only asked because you were wrong on the dialect last time — table two. Somerset.

Sam I wonder why people never laugh at my place and chips joke?

Bill Not funny?

Sam Too subtle. I'm sure table three are from Suffolk and I will confirm, if it pleases you.

Bill Are you ever going to put your little study of dialects to some use?

Sam Yes. I may write a book.

Bill A book? Hah!

Sam Books on English dialects are almost non-existent. Did you know that?

Bill What happened about your study of sea birds? We hear nothing of that.

Sam My dear Bill, when the holiday season finishes I shall start on the birds again. And I'll remind you, I've seen most of the world's sea birds in their natural habitat. Not just Australia and the Isle of Man.

Bill There's nothing wrong with the Isle of Man.

They complete the order and put everything on a tray

Sam Now you take the tray and see if you agree — table three is Suffolk.

Bill (*picking up the tray*) You could be wrong.

Sam Is there a bet?

Bill No, I never win. (*He moves to the café door*) By the way, it's your throw — on the Ludo.

Bill exits into the café

Sam hurries into the living-room and examines the Ludo board. He picks up the Ludo cup, then shakes and throws the dice

Sam Five. (*He moves a counter, audibly counting to five*) Um … that's a good move. (*He returns to the kitchen and begins washing up*) Well?

Bill enters from the café carrying the tray and an order

Bill Norfolk.

Sam Norfolk? Rubbish. How d'you know that?
Bill I asked them.
Sam That's cheating.
Bill It's not cheating because it's not a game.
Sam Everything is a game!
Bill Table one: two cheese and biscuits. (*He puts the order on hook one*)
Sam Right. Cheddar?
Bill Gloucester. You're wrong again. (*He prepares the cheese and biscuits during the following*)
Sam And talking of games, I shook a five on the Ludo.
Bill Five. What was your move?
Sam Blue four to blue nine.
Bill (*considering*) Um … no danger there.
Sam Don't be too sure about that.
Bill (*glancing through the café window*) That girl on table six …
Sam One coffee and she's been here an hour ...
Bill Only a child.
Sam Pretty girl.
Bill Waiting for somebody?
Sam Killing time?
Bill It's late to be killing time.
Sam (*looking at his watch*) Nearing nine o'clock.
Bill Is that all? My legs say eleven o'clock. I believe my legs are twice as old as I am.
Sam Nonsense.
Bill They are certainly getting too old for this business. You never seem to be tired.
Sam I do, often, but one can be weary and happy at the same time.

Linda appears at the café door. She is wearing well-worn trendy clothes and carrying a much-used holdall bag

Linda Hi there! All right, then?
Bill Oh! (*He exchanges a look with Sam*)
Sam Something we can do for you?
Linda I want to pay the bill.
Sam We usually bring the bill to the table.
Linda That's all right. Save you leggin' it.
Sam (*moving to the hook board and taking table six's bill down*) Table six: one coffee. Will there be anything else?
Linda Shouldn't think so. (*She takes the bill from Sam without looking at it*) D'you know, I've been sorting you two. (*She moves into the room and places her bag on the floor*)

Sam Sorting? You mean watching?

Linda I was in here last night.

Bill We remember … (*He looks at Sam*)

Sam One coffee and packet of biscuits.

Linda Fancy you remembering that.

Sam And you were here for an hour.

Linda And clocking me as well!

Sam Skill of the trade.

Linda Well, I'll tell you … You two old fellas — not to be too unkind — I'd rate you two a tad over the top for this kind of thing, cafés and that. I've done a bit of waiting at tables m'self, and d'you know what I reckon? I reckon you need me.

Sam And what makes you think we need you?

Linda Well. You're both knocking on a bit, and you need a pair of young legs to speed the place up.

Sam This is not a fast food joint, young lady. It's a place for leisurely eating. One may take an hour drinking a cup of coffee, as you well know. And another thing: don't knock old legs. Old legs can knock on their own. I take it you're looking for a job?

Linda Right. Have you got one?

Bill (*coming in quickly*) No.

Sam (*after a thought*) I don't think we have.

Linda Why not?

Sam What d'you mean, why not? Because we can get along without you very well — that's why not. (*Calmly*) Why don't you be a nice young lady and pay your bill for the coffee and make your way home.

Linda (*staring at Sam*) I can't do that.

Sam Can't do what?

Linda Either of it. Pay the bill or go home. I've got no money and nowhere to go.

Sam Ah.

Sam and Bill exchange a look

Bill (*picking up the tray*) Excuse me. I must attend to the customers. Two cheese and biscuits. Table … ?

Sam Yes! Table one.

Bill heads into the café. Linda steps further into the kitchen to allow him to pass

Bill exits

Linda I've had experience you know.

Sam Oh, I'm sure you have. At what, exactly?

Linda Are you being crude? I hope not! I'm not that kind of girl …

Sam Of course not. But don't try intimidating me, young lady. I've been through it all before in all parts of the world, with ladies of far more experience and guile.

Linda (*retaliating*) You're bloody quaint, you are.

Sam (*countering, not heavily*) That's bloody true, that is. (*Pause*) What next?

Linda What?

Sam What shall we say next? It's your move.

Linda (*deflated*) I don't know, do I!

They laugh and the tension falls away. Sam cuts a piece of cheese and hands it to Linda

Are you going to give me a job?

Sam There must be jobs in town.

Linda It's the end of the holiday season. They're sacking waitresses.

Sam What about your home? You have a home. East, west, home's best.

Linda I've left home. I don't care about being paid, that's all. I'll do the washing up, anything. Tomorrow I'm moving in with a friend.

Sam Can't you move in tonight?

Linda No, he's got someone with him. She's moving out tomorrow. She's been with him all the summer and now she's going back to Hemel Hempstead — for the winter.

Sam Wintering in Hemel Hempstead? That sounds exciting. And you're going to winter here.

Linda Right.

Sam Who is this friend? Would I know him?

Linda Just a guy. (*She changes the subject*) I slept on the beach last night.

Sam The beach? On your own?

Linda Yes, and it was bloody cold, I can tell you.

Sam Stop! Let me guess.

Linda What?

Sam You're from Battersea.

Linda Battersea? No! I was brought up in Lewisham.

Sam Well, there you are. I was nearly right. I'm a student of dialects and places.

Linda You're a bit old to be a student.

Sam One is never too old to be a student. And I'm not old.

Linda Sorr-ee!

Bill enters from the café

Bill Table two want to pay.
Sam Right. Bill, I have to tell you ... (*To Linda*) I'm sorry, I don't know your name.
Linda Linda.
Sam Linda. I like that. Linda insists she's from Lewisham, but we know better. She's from Battersea.
Linda I am not.
Bill Does it matter?
Sam Only to students of dialect. The young lady is looking for somewhere to rest her weary head.
Bill Rest? To sleep? There's no room here.
Sam That's true. (*To Linda*) He's right.
Linda I can sleep on the floor, or anywhere. I've got a sleeping bag.
Sam She slept on the beach last night.
Bill Not here. I don't like it.
Sam She's not asking you to like it.
Bill So, you're going to let her stay here?
Sam I haven't said that, not specifically. The customers come first — at least those who have money. (*He smiles at Linda*) The bill for table two?
Bill Yes. table two.
Sam (*taking the bill from its hook*) Done!

Sam exits into the café

There is an uncomfortable pause. Bill avoids looking at Linda. He moves used crockery to the draining board and remains at the sink, picking up a handful of cutlery. Linda moves closer to Bill who is unaware of the move

Linda (*shouting*) Boo!
Bill (*startled*) Oh, my God! (*He drops the cutlery into the sink, causing a loud clatter*)

Linda laughs

Why did you do that?
Linda Sorry! Sorry! Did I startle you?
Bill Yes, you did.
Linda Sorry. But you wouldn't look at me.
Bill Is that some sort of crime? You could have killed me.
Linda (*amused*) Don't be daft. I didn't touch you.

Sam enters from the café

Sam What's happening in here?
Linda Nothing.
Sam I heard shouting — and a clatter.
Linda Just a little game. Right?
Sam Bill?
Bill That's right. Just a game.
Sam Shouts and clatters?
Linda My fault. I'm sorry. I'll be going. (*She picks up her bag and begins to move to the exit*)
Sam Stop. Stop.

Sam takes Linda's arm and stops her. He lets go of her

Now let's get one or two things straight, shall we?
Linda What things?
Sam How old are you?
Linda (*after a hesitation*) Eighteen.
Sam Are you in any kind of trouble?
Linda No.
Sam Nowhere to sleep is your only problem.
Linda Basic ... Yes.
Sam Basically ... Right! If you'll kindly go into our small living-room — (*He takes her arm*) Bill and I will convene a meeting in the kitchen here. (*He leads Linda into the living-room*) This way.
Linda I can walk on my own, thanks very much.
Sam Make yourself at home. (*He returns to the kitchen, closing the door behind him*) I think we should let her stay — for one night.
Bill Well, I'm sorry, Sam, but I don't. She frightened me nearly to death just now.
Sam Women have always frightened you, and yet you married twice. I've never understood that.
Bill If you're going to ask me what I think — and I don't think you are — or maybe you are ... I don't know. Are you?
Sam Well, say it.
Bill It's not right for us to take a young girl off the street and let her sleep here with us.
Sam I would have thought sleeping with us would have been her safest place. She can sleep in the living-room — in her sleeping bag. But I wouldn't let her do that unless you agree.
Bill I don't agree. I wouldn't want anything to change. I believe it was fate brought us together after all those years. Let's avoid complications and grow old quietly.
Sam I will not grow old quietly — and she's not a complication.
Bill She's a complication to me.

Sam (*looking at his watch*) All right. It's now nearing ten o'clock, and quite dark outside and not very warm. Will you tell her to go?
Bill No. I thought you would be the one ... .
Sam No, no. Not me. I would be the one to ask her to stay. You must be the one to ask her to go.
Bill I don't think that's fair.
Sam I think it's perfectly fair.
Bill No. (*He considers*) All right, I'll do it.
Sam Good for you.
Bill I will.
Sam Good.
Bill I'll tell her. I'll tell her that she must leave.
Sam Right.
Bill I'm not afraid to do that.
Sam I know.
Bill I shall be very polite.
Sam Of course you will.
Bill Courteous — and perfectly calm.
Sam Of course you will.
Bill (*after a pause*) Will you excuse me?

Bill moves to the living-room door, hesitates, then enters

Linda (*cheerfully*) Hallo. All right, then?
Bill (*nervously*) Yes ... well ... Hallo. (*He closes the door*)

Sam moves to listen briefly at the living-room door

Linda I'm sorry if I frightened you in there.
Bill You didn't really frighten me.
Linda Didn't I? I thought I did.
Bill No, no.

Sam moves from the door and exits into the café

Linda Good. (*Short pause*) Do you have something to tell me?
Bill Um? Oh, yes.
Linda You're going to tell me I can't stay.
Bill Well, yes — and no.
Linda That makes a lot of sense.
Bill (*uneasily*) I — er ... (*Pause*) Do you play tiddly-winks?
Linda Tiddly-winks?
Bill Yes.

Linda I've played a bit when I was a kid. Why?

Bill That's good! Good! (*He produces a boxed game of tiddly-winks from a drawer*) We play a lot of games here — as you can see.

Linda That's nice.

Bill (*placing the box on the table*) That's the tiddly-winks box. (*He moves awkwardly from the living-room to the kitchen. He closes the door and heaves a sigh of relief*)

Linda, puzzled, cautiously opens the box

Sam enters from the café

Sam Table four are from South Wales. I'll mark that down. (*He puts the tray down and crosses to his notebook*) Cardiff, I would guess. But I will confirm.

Bill She plays tiddly-winks.

Sam Who? Does she now! How d'you know that?

Bill I asked her.

Sam Well, there you are. Has she gone?

Bill No. She can stay just one night — if you agree.

Sam And you've told her.

Bill No.

Sam Then what happened?

Bill We talked, that's all.

Sam What about?

Bill Tiddly-winks, mainly.

Sam Tiddly-winks? Shall I talk to her?

Bill Just one night — that is all.

Sam (*moving to the living-room door*) One night, that is all. (*He enters the living-room*) Well, young lady, this is your lucky day.

Linda Oh, it's you this time.

Sam Yes, it's me. We've decided to let you stay.

Linda Thanks. To play tiddly-winks?

Sam Yes, if you like.

Linda Ooo! That's kinky — tiddlying and winking.

Sam What other games d'you play? We have Ludo, snakes and ladders, Lexicon, dominoes, draughts … .

Linda Whatever turns you on. I've played them a bit — when I was a kid.

Sam You're still a kid.

Linda (*indignantly*) I am not.

Sam Now that is sad — because I am.

Linda You are quaint! D'you know that?

Sam shrugs

They talk a lot about you two in the town.

Sam Do they now.

Linda My friend told me, you've been here just two years. He said you'd never done this sort of thing before — cafés and that.

Sam That's right. And it's not a café. I don't like that word. It doesn't adequately describe an establishment such as this. We're a bit above a café. I'm trying to find the right word.

Linda You've left it a bit late to start. What were you doing before?

Sam Most things — in most places.

Linda Such as what?

Sam Such as you're asking too many questions.

Linda I'm like that. What d'you want me to do? Washing-up?

Sam Nothing.

Linda Nuffink?

Sam Nothing.

Linda Leave it out, Grandad. A deal's a deal. I work for my sleep.

Sam Please don't call me Grandad. My name is Sam. (*After a thought*) I shall call you Lewisham.

Linda Lewisham. (*Pause*) Whatever turns you on.

Sam To work then, Lewisham. Follow me. It's washing-up time for you.

Linda Yes, sir! Sam, sir! (*She salutes*)

Sam leads Linda into the kitchen

CURTAIN

SCENE 2

The same. Four days later. 8 a.m.

When the CURTAIN *rises, the living-room is in semi-darkness, with the morning sun coming through the drawn curtains. On the floor, Linda is turning restlessly in her sleeping bag*

There are no orders on the order board in the kitchen. Bill is in the kitchen, working as quietly as possible. He fills a kettle and begins preparing tea.

Linda draws herself from the sleeping bag. She is wearing a man's pyjama top which covers her briefs. She crosses the room and opens the curtains. Sunlight floods in. She enters the kitchen

Linda (*cheerfully*) Hi there, Bill.

Bill (*nervously*) Oh — er — good-morning.

Linda You're up early.

Bill It's my usual time.

Linda (*playfully*) Shall I make the tea?

Bill No. It's all right.

Linda I made it yesterday — and the morning before.

Bill I always make the tea. Always do. Always have done.

Linda Sorry for speaking, I'm sure. (*She smiles*) Why are you so nervous of me?

Bill Why should I be nervous of you?

Linda I don't know, do I. Let me help. I'll get the mugs. (*She collects mugs from the shelf*)

Bill I can manage.

Linda You don't like me kipping here, do you?

Bill I wouldn't say that. But it has been longer than you said.

Linda It's been three nights. I'm sorry about that. But last night was the last night.

Bill You said that yesterday.

Linda It's taking longer than I thought. Sorry. Anyway, you can always kick me out.

Bill I'm sure that won't be necessary — if you have difficulties.

Linda I don't have difficulties. I'm helping you out in the caff, that's what I'm doing; working my fingers to the bone and killing m'feet at the same time. But I enjoy it. (*She kisses Bill on the cheek*) There you are. The kettle's boiling. Have you put the tea in the pot?

Bill (*touching his cheek*) No.

Linda Come on! What have you been doing? I know — you've been looking at my legs.

Bill (*embarrassed*) I have not.

Linda You've seen girls' legs before, surely. We've all got them. (*She lifts the pyjama top*) See?

Bill I'm aware of that.

Linda Well, that's something. D'you still fancy girls at your age?

Bill Pardon?

Sam descends the stairs to the living-room

Linda You heard, you cheeky old devil.

Bill I'm not answering your questions.

Linda Perhaps I should get dressed. How old do men get before they stop fancying girls?

Bill I'm not answering.

Sam enters the kitchen from the living-room

Sam Good-morning, Bill. Good-morning, Lewisham.

Linda Good-morning, Sam.

Sam (*to Linda*) And you're walking about with nothing on again.

Linda I've got something on.

Sam But only just.

Linda Shall I pour the tea?

Bill No.

Linda Yes, I will. I like pouring tea. (*She begins pouring the tea*) I always made morning tea for my nan ... (*She stops*)

Sam Nan? Who is Nan?

Linda Nobody.

Sam (*persisting*) You said "Nan". You let that one slip out. Is Nan someone at home?

Linda No questions. You promised.

Sam It wouldn't be your sister ——

Linda ignores this

I know! You had a nanny!

Linda Don't be daft. Who d'you think I am? (*She pours tea; reflectively*) I always called my gran Nan. Always have, ever since I can remember.

Sam We all have a granny or two ... .

Linda She brought me up, my nan.

Sam Don't you mean "brung" you up?

Pause

Linda I shall miss this place, I really will — and you two old codgers. (*She recovers*) But I'm leaving today, you'll be pleased to hear.

Sam We're not pleased to hear that at all, are we, Bill?

Linda Bill is pleased, I'm sure.

Bill (*to Linda*) Well ... I know what you mean, and I know what he means — if you know what I mean.

Linda Well, Bill, that makes a lot of sense.

Bill It's nothing personal, you understand.

Linda (*teasingly*) Bill, I know that. It's a heavy, heavy risk I've taken here. (*She gives Bill a motherly hug*) But I've trusted you. I knew you'd keep your sexy feelings under wraps.

Bill swallows hard

Anyway, it doesn't matter. Today is my leaving day. Can I use your phone later?

Sam Yes. Who are you going to ring? Your nan?

Linda No my friend, of course. He said to ring him today. Your tea, gentlemen!

Linda hands mugs of tea to Sam and Bill

(*Sipping her tea*) Ummm … Nothing like a good cup of tea.

Sam And this is nothing like a good cup of tea. Now, who exactly is this friend of yours?

Linda No more questions. Drink your tea. (*She moves into the living-room*)

Sam (*following Linda*) Surely you can tell us?

Linda None of your business.

Bill (*following Sam*) Leave her alone. We have work to do.

Linda Yes, you have. Can I help?

Bill No, I don't think so. This is the morning we settle our account at the market.

Sam Do you have the list?

Bill Yes.

Linda Then I'll get the breakfast. What's it to be? Not bran again?

Sam Yes, plenty of roughage. Good for the bowels.

Linda You two must have the best bowels in town.

Sam You're right. We've won prizes at the flower show.

Linda What? (*She laughs*) No!

Sam Best pair of bowels in the Senior Class.

Bill Please, Sam! (*To Linda*) It will not be necessary to get the breakfast. I'll do it when we get back.

Sam It's time we were on our way.

Bill and Sam swig their tea and place their mugs on the table

(*To Linda*) And you be good, and ——

Linda ⎫
          ⎬ (*together*) — if you can't be good, be careful!
Sam   ⎭

Linda I know! And if you can't be careful, be good at it. Right? (*She laughs*)

Sam Every time! We won't be long!

Bill is not amused

Bill and Sam exit into the street

The laughter fades from Linda's face. She places her mug on the table and contemplates the phone. She lifts the receiver and dials a number

Linda Hallo? ... Oh! Are you still there? ... It doesn't matter who I am. Why
haven't you cleared off to Hemel Hempstead? ... It is my business! ... You
cheeky cow! Is Vince there? I want to speak to him .... Then where is he?
He's never out of bed at this time. Well, you can tell him this from me: I'm
sick —— (*The receiver has been slammed down at the other end. Linda
slowly moves the receiver from her ear and slams it down heavily. She
crosses angrily to the table and collects the mugs*) What he sees in her, I'll
never bleedin' know. She's all wrinkles, mascara and polyfilla and paint.
(*She stamps into the kitchen carrying the mugs, puts them noisily into the
sink, turns on the tap, and picks up the washing-up liquid bottle*)

There is a knock on the street door

Who the hell is that! (*She hammers the washing-up liquid bottle on to the
drainer, strides aggressively into the living-room and opens the street
door*)

Connie is on the doorstep

Nan!
Connie So there you are! (*She moves into the room*)
Linda Nan!
Connie Yes, Nan.
Linda What are you doing here?
Connie What d'you think I'm doing here? Selling buttons?
Linda (*closing the door*) I can't believe it.
Connie I bet you can't, my girl.
Linda How did you know I was here?
Connie Never mind that. What's going on?
Linda Nothing's going on.
Connie I can see that. Everything's coming off, by the look of you. Get some
clothes on. (*She glances into the kitchen*) Who's in there?
Linda Nobody. How did you get here?
Connie By train. I came down last night. They tell me this place is owned
by two men.
Linda That's right.
Connie You're living here with two men. That's disgusting.
Linda It's not disgusting. They're two very nice old guys.
Connie Old men? That's even more disgusting. How old?
Linda About your age.
Connie (*indignantly*) What d'you mean — my age? I'm not old.
Linda Well, there you are! There's no pleasing you. What d'you want,
coming here?

Connie I'm taking you home, my girl, that's what I'm doing.

Linda No, you're not.

Connie Oh, but I am.

Linda Why?

Connie You know damn well why. You ran away from me.

Linda I did not run away.

Connie Well, you could have fooled me, darling. I've heard nothing from you for four months.

Linda I told you I was going.

Connie I didn't think you meant it, did I? I thought you were joking.

Linda Now you know I wasn't joking.

Connie So why did you run away?

Linda I didn't run. I told you, I just packed my bag and left — walking, not running.

Connie When I wasn't looking.

Linda Your fault. You were never looking at me.

Connie I have a pub to run. The pub is my living. Blimey, I have to live, don't I?

Linda Right! Now I have to find my way to live.

Connie (*looking up the stairs*) And what a way to start. Where have you been sleeping?

Linda There, on the floor. In the sleeping bag.

Sam enters the living-room from the street

Sam Oh! (*He closes the door*) What's going on here?

Connie That's a good question.

Linda (*cheerfully*) Hallo, Sam.

Sam What's happening? Something wrong?

Connie (*to Linda*) Who is this?

Linda This is Sam. He lives here.

Connie So this is one of them.

Sam Am I? One of what?

Linda (*interceding*) You're back quick. What happened?

Sam We forgot the cheque book. (*He makes to move away and find the cheque book*)

Linda Sam, this is my nan.

Sam Your nan! Oh! I – er – didn't know that. I'm very pleased to meet you.

Connie And I want to know what you're doing with my granddaughter.

Sam I'm doing nothing with your granddaughter. Lewisham is working here.

Connie Lewisham?

Linda (*cheerfully*) That's what they call me.

Connie That's where you live — Lewisham.
Linda I know that, don't I?
Connie Her name's Linda, and I'm taking her home.
Sam Well, you can please yourself about that.
Linda I'm not going home.
Sam (*to Linda*) And you can please yourself as well.
Linda Thanks very much!
Connie (*to Sam*) You have no right keeping her here. She's under age.
Sam (*to Linda*) You said you were eighteen.
Linda Well — nearly.
Connie You're only seventeen. Did she tell you she's run away from home?
Sam Yes, she did.
Linda You told me to clear off.
Connie I did not.
Linda Yes you did. You were always telling to me clear off. You said I was a blooming nuisance.
Connie And so you were.
Linda Well, there you are.
Connie It's a figure of speech, that's all.

Bill enters from the street. He does not see Connie at first

Bill (*to Sam*) Come on. What's keeping you? (*He sees Connie*) Oh! ... Hallo.
Linda Bill, this is my nan.
Bill (*nervously*) Is it? Good Lord!
Linda Nan, this is Bill.
Connie Are you the other one?
Bill Other one?
Connie The other one harbouring my granddaughter.
Bill Harbouring?
Connie Yes ... (*Pause*) Har-bour-ing. (*The word stretches then fades on her lips. She studies Bill and Sam in turn and shows some distress*)
Linda (*concerned*) Nan?

No response

Nan? What's the matter?
Connie (*vacantly*) Nothing.
Linda Nan, are you ill?
Connie (*still looking at Sam and Bill*) I'm not sure.
Sam Will you sit down?
Connie No. No, I'm all right. (*Pause*) Yes, perhaps I will. (*She sits*) Thank you, Mr ... Mr ...?

Sam Would you like a drink of some kind? Water?
Connie No, thank you.
Sam Something stronger?
Connie Whisky?
Sam Whisky. (*To Bill*) Whisky.
Bill Yes, whisky. (*He prepares a glass of whisky*)
Connie Thank you, Mr … ?
Sam Sam. Just Sam.
Connie (*recovering*) That seems very personal. I never like Christian names straight away, never have. I'm Mrs Tozer. What's your surname?
Sam It doesn't really matter about that.
Connie Oh, but I'm sure it does, dear. Now what is it?

Bill heads towards Connie with the whisky

Sam (*hesitating*) It's — er — Ellis.

Sam exchanges a look with Bill

Connie Ellis?
Sam Yes.

Bill hands the whisky to Sam

Your whisky.

Sam hands the whisky to Connie

Connie Thank you. (*She drinks*)
Linda Nan, what happened? Did you feel faint or something?
Connie Yes — or something. But I feel a little better now.
Sam Good. Now you stay there. I'm sure you have things to talk about. We have a little business to finish — just down the road. Feel free to stay as long as you wish. (*To Linda*) You'll be all right looking after her?
Linda Yes.
Bill Or, if you have both gone when we get back, we'll understand. Just slam the door.
Linda Don't worry, Bill. I'll still be here.
Bill (*disappointedly*) Oh.

Bill exits into the street

Sam See you later.

Sam exits

Connie stands, and stares thoughtfully at the street door

Connie What d'you know about those two?
Linda Nan, are you all right?
Connie Yes.
Linda How did you know I was here ——
Connie Um ... ?
Linda — in this place? (*Pause*) Nan?
Connie (*vaguely*) What? (*Dismissively*) Oh, it was Hilda Simpson. What d'you know about those two?
Linda Sam and Bill? Not a lot. I've only been here three days. What about Hilda Simpson?
Connie She was here on holiday. She saw you here — and rang me.
Linda I'm not coming home with you.
Connie It doesn't matter about that now. Is there a telephone here? (*She sees the telephone*) Ah, there it is. What were you doing when I came in?
Linda Washing up. Getting the breakfast.
Connie Then get along and do it, there's a good girl.

Connie moves Linda into the kitchen during the following

  Go on.
Linda 'Ere, ease off. Stop pushing me round.
Connie Go on, go on. I have to make an urgent phone call.
Linda What about?
Connie Mind your nose, darling. Mind your nose.

Connie closes the door on a puzzled-looking Linda, crosses to the telephone and dials a number. Linda remains by the door. listening

Connie (*into the phone*) Hallo. ... Is that you, Winifred? ... . It's me. ... Connie, of course. ... (*Louder*) Connie! ... I know I'm faint. That's because I'm whispering! ... (*Louder*) I'm whispering! Now listen carefully. There's ... Yes, I got here all right ... (*Impatiently*) Yes, I've found Linda; but there's something I have to tell you ... Yes, yes, she's all right, but it doesn't matter about Linda. ... I said it doesn't matter. Will you shut up and listen. You'll never guess who I think I've found — down here. George and Arthur. ... The very same. ... No, they're not dead. They're very much alive. ... I know it's forty years on, but I'd know those two bastards anywhere. Now, listen. I want you to pack a bag and get here on the next train. ... Yes, today ... Having your feet done isn't important. It doesn't matter about your bloody chiropodist. Cancel him. (*She looks at the kitchen door*) Just hold the line. (*She puts the receiver down, moves to the kitchen* *door and opens it. To Linda*) I knew you'd be listening, you nosey cow.

Linda Moo! What's going on?

Connie Nothing's going on. Get on with your work. Go on. (*She closes the door and returns to the phone*) Winifred? … I'll ring you again from my hotel. … Yes. Stay near the phone. … Goodbye. (*She replaces the receiver and opens the kitchen door*) I'm going now.

Linda Where?

Connie Never mind. "Where" is my business.

Linda What about me?

Connie (*pleasantly*) You have work to do. I suggest you stay here and get on with it. You'll be seeing me again, have no fear about that one, darling.

Connie exits into the street

Linda moves slowly from the kitchen into the living-room and looks pensively at the street door. She turns to look at the telephone, then picks up the receiver. She hesitates, then dials

Linda Vince? It's me. … Linda. I rang earlier. … Am I coming around today? … Yes, you did. … You said she was going today! … So, what am I going to do? I can't stay here. … Something's happened. … Now you're saying it's tomorrow again. It's always tomorrow … (*She softens*) Yes … Well, if you say so. … D'you really mean that? … All right. (*She replaces the receiver*)

Sam enters from the street

Sam Lewisham.

Linda (*sadly*) Oh, it's you.

Sam I've just seen your nan crossing the street. What happened?

Linda (*evasively*) Nothing happened. She seemed to lose interest in me for some reason. She went a bit strange.

Sam I thought she had a funny look on her face when she came out of the door. I was in Sid's fishing tackle shop.

Linda What were you doing there?

Sam Just keeping an eye on things here.

Linda You were spying?

Sam Just watching.

Linda Watching from Sid's fishing shop. Proper little James bleedin' Bond, aren't you?

Bill enters

Hallo, Bill.

Bill (*seeing Linda*) Oh! You're still here!

Linda 'Fraid so, Bill. You can't blow me away that easy.

Sam (*to Bill*) It seems Nan's gone a little strange and left.

Bill (*to Linda*) She didn't take you with her?

Linda I'm still here. Sorry about that, Bill.

Bill (*grunting*) I'll get the breakfast. Have you washed up?

Linda Nearly. I'll finish it off now.

Bill No, thank you. I can do it perfectly well on my own. (*He heads for the kitchen*)

Linda (*lightly*) Well, be like that then. I just thought I'd help. I want to go to the loo anyway — I'm bursting for a piddle.

Bill "tut-tut"s

All right? (*She heads for the stairs*)

Sam Have you made your phone call?

Linda Yes, I have.

Sam So are you moving in today, with whoever it is?

Linda I'm not sure. But it doesn't matter. I'll sort it out.

Bill collects a table-cloth from the kitchen, returns to the living-room and puts the cloth on the table during the following

Sam I'll say this: if you want to stay here another night, it will be all right with — er — us.

Bill gives Sam a look

Linda I said I was going today. Remember? (*She returns to Sam and kisses him on the cheek*) Thanks anyway. (*To Bill*) You got a kiss earlier. You're not getting another; you'll get too excited. (*She crosses her legs*) Ooo! I must go — I'll wet m'self.

Linda hurries up the stairs and exits

Bill Why did you say she could stay another night? This has gone on long enough, I think.

Sam Bill, she's very young.

Bill Being young is not a licence. It's not a concession for rudeness or — or disrespect. I don't like it. (*He moves into the kitchen*)

Sam Oh, dear. (*He follows Bill*) You're getting grumpy again.

Bill She's too old for her age, that's what I say, too old by far. (*He sets to work preparing for breakfast, collecting up cereal, dishes, milk, mugs etc. on to a tray and switching on the kettle during the following*)

Sam You never had any children. Married twice and no children.

Bill I never liked children.

Sam Sad, that. (*He contributes to the preparations during the following*) Your second marriage must have been ... how long?

Bill Twenty-two years. And we don't talk of that. And what about you? You had no children.

Sam Well, none that I would own up to. There could be a few around the world, dotted here and there.

Bill Before your travels, you were married for three years.

Sam No time for children with Connie. Lucky there. Lucky for the children, that is. I got out and away just in time. Three years married was long enough.

Bill Connie was all right. (*He carries the tray into the living room*)

Sam (*following Bill*) I'm glad you think so. Is it my turn on the Ludo?

Bill Yes.

Sam moves to the Ludo board. Bill unloads the tray and arranges the table setting

People are already talking. A young girl staying here with two old men. If they see her dressed as she was this morning.

Sam Ah ... .

Bill I feel uneasy with her here. I wish it were just the two of us; that's all.

Sam (*shaking and throwing the dice*) Three. She enjoys playing Ludo. Have you noticed that?

Bill (*glancing towards the stairs*) I'll make the tea.

Sam Just a moment. (*He moves a counter*) One, two, three and we'll all have tea.

Bill looks at Sam's Ludo move then heads for the kitchen

Bill That's a wrong move. (*He enters the kitchen and makes a pot of tea during the following*)

Sam (*shouting*) I don't think so.

Linda descends the stairs

Linda What have you two been talking about down here?

Sam Man's talk.

Linda Oh. It's a pity Bill doesn't like me.

Sam Of course he likes you.

Linda Mind you, I don't blame him. I'm not a very nice person to know.

Sam I wouldn't say that. You try very hard at being — not a very nice person — but it doesn't really work.

Linda What d'you mean?

Sam Not on me, it doesn't. I've met a few hard ladies in my time, real shockers. You're not in their league, nowhere near.

Bill (*entering the living-room, carrying the teapot*) I've made the tea.

Sam and Bill sit at the table and pour cereal into bowls

Linda Ooo! (*She returns to the table*) I think I'll have some Bran Flakes this morning. I'm a bit bunged up. (*She sits at the table and pours herself some Bran Flakes*)

Bill Please!

Linda Well, it does keep the bowels going. You told me that.

Bill He told you that.

Linda Sorry. (*She stands up*) Shall I pour the milk?

Bill Thank you, but I'll pour my own milk. You put too much in yesterday.

Linda Sorry.

Bill It was too mulchy.

Linda Oh, dear. (*To Sam*) What about you?

Sam As it comes.

Linda Here it comes — from a great height.

Linda pours milk into Sam's bowl and hands the jug to Bill. Bill pours his milk and they begin eating

Sam What I want to know from you is this ... .

Linda Is what?

Sam Are you going home with Nan?

Linda No way.

Sam So who is it you're moving in with today?

Linda I told you: that question is banned. Don't keep on. (*Pause*) All right, all right, I'll tell you. (*Pause*) D'you know Vincent?

Sam Vincent, who works in that bloody awful amusement arcade?

Linda That's him.

Sam You're not moving in with him. You must be mad. He must be at least thirty-five and no good. He's a rake.

Linda (*amused*) A rake? He's not thin.

Sam (*to Bill*) You know Vincent. Last year he called himself Arnold and worked on the beach with the deck chairs.

Bill Arnold! Oh, dear.

Linda Arnold?

Sam That's him. Last year he was literature — Arnold Bennett. This year it's painting — Vincent Van Gogh. If you want my advice ——

Linda (*sharply*) I don't want your advice, thank you.

Sam I was only going to say ——

Linda Shut up! Don't say it!

There is silence. Bill and Sam continue eating

I don't like this bran stuff. It's like eating cardboard. (*She pushes the dish aside*) Hey! You're always asking me questions. Why don't I ask you some?

Sam Why not? You may not get an answer.

Linda Right.

Sam Right.

Linda (*thinking*) OK. What I want to know is ... (*pause*) are you two a couple of old queens?

Sam and Bill choke on their Bran Flakes

Sam You cheeky little madam!

Linda (*standing up*) Well are you or not?

Sam No!

Bill No! Indeed we're not!

Sam I've been married.

Linda Don't spit everywhere.

Bill And I've been married twice!

Linda Anyway you could be married to each other.

Sam (*emphatically*) We are brothers!

Linda Brothers?

Bill Yes. He's my brother. I'm his brother.

Linda Straight up? You don't look like brothers. You don't behave like brothers.

Bill There's a reason for that.

Linda What's that then?

Bill (*after a hesitation*) My brother — and myself — met just over two years ago, having not seen each other for nearly forty years.

Linda Is that right!

Sam That's right. I don't see why we should explain any more.

Linda 'Ere, have you two got something murky to hide?

Bill (*continuing, anxiously*) No, we have nothing to hide. (*He stands and loads the tray during the following*)

Linda Good. Forty years that's a long time. How did you meet? At a funeral? Funerals are good places for meeting relations. That's what my nan says.

Bill Not a funeral.

Linda And you met and started this little place. That's a turn up. What about your wives?

Sam and Bill exchange a look. Bill carries the loaded tray into the kitchen

Sam No more questions.

Linda I never had a brother or a sister. Wish I did. Funny things, families: ours is anyway. I never knew my mum and dad. They split up and cleared off when I was three. I've always lived with my nan — since I can remember. (*She laughs*) She wanted me to go on the stage. That's all I was any good at, at school — acting.

Sam Now I can believe that.

Bill returns

Linda Nan sent me to elocution lessons — you must've noticed listening to me — and dancing lessons.

Bill (*with sudden interest*) Dancing?

Sam Dancing! Now you've woken Bill. Bill was a dancer.

Linda Is that right? Were you, Bill?

Bill As a young man, I did a bit.

Sam He did a lot.

Linda Hated speech and drama, but the dancing was way out.

Sam He was a professional.

Linda Bill? A professional dancer?

Bill Well — in the chorus. Musicals, that sort of thing.

Linda Blimey! I wouldn't have guessed that of you, Bill. I like tap dancing best of all.

Bill Tap! Show me a few steps.

Linda What now?

Sam Why not?

Linda (*after considering*) All right. Not without shoes. I'll have to put my shoes on. (*She picks up her shoes*) They're no good for dancing. (*She puts her shoes on*)

Sam They'll do.

Linda Better than bare feet. You can't tap dance in bare feet —unless your toe nails are long.

Linda Do you know *Sunny Side of the Street*?

Bill Course I know *Sunny Side of the Street.*

Linda I'll do that then. I'm not sure that I can remember anything properly. (*She stands up*) Let me think now.

Linda "dah dee dah's" "On the Sunny Side of the Street" in tempo, and performs a short tap sequence

Bill I know that step.

Linda Do you? Well, it's pretty basic. Do it with me then. Will you? Come on, Bill!

Linda takes Bill's hand

Sam Go on, Bill.
Bill (*considering*) I'll have a try. (*He stands and flexes his ankles*) Loosen
    the ankles.
Linda That's right then, twinkle toes. Ready?
Bill Ready.
Linda Take it away, Bill.

*Linda sings and, with Bill, performs a tap dance sequence. Sam cheers and
applauds*

    Hey, that was good.
Sam It was!
Linda (*to Bill*) Let's do a finish?
Bill Why not.

*They perform a "twirl" and a bow, Bill bending Linda backwards over his
arm. Sam cheers and applauds*

    The street door opens and Connie enters

*Bill drops Linda to the floor. Connie moves in and stands looking at the prone
body of Linda*

CURTAIN

SCENE 3

The following day. It is late morning

*The busy lunchtime period is yet to arrive, but when it does there will be many
small jobs to be carried out between the preparation of the meals, such as
washing up, wiping surfaces, keeping kettles filled and close to boiling,
putting away cups, saucers, plates etc. The orders pierced on the board are
regularly consulted*

*When the CURTAIN rises, there are no orders on the order board. Bill is
making final preparations in the kitchen. The timer on the microwave
"pings". He takes six jacket potatoes from the microwave and places them
in the cooker*

Sam enters, carrying an empty tray and an order

Sam First order of the day. Table five … (*He stops and looks through the window into the café*)

Bill I'm transferring spuds to the cooker.

Sam Their dialect could be anywhere south of Oxford. A sort of middle class noisy. One cheddar cheese salad and one "Today's Special".

Bill Really? Who would want a fish pie at this time of the morning?

Sam It's not fish pie. It's tuna flan. (*He collects two plates and puts them on the work surface*)

Bill I don't like fish when it's mucked about.

Sam Mucked about? What d'you mean, mucked about? (*He takes a flan from the fridge*) You lack any kind of imagination. That's what comes of living in Australia and the Isle of Man; neither of which is a watershed of culinary adventure. This tuna flan looks absolutely wonderful! (*He places the flan on the work surface*)

Bill (*taking some cheese from the cheeseboard*) Why are you so enthusiastic about everything? It's not natural at our age.

Sam (*cutting the flan*) Ah, but age is the spur. I'm trying to keep up with the world.

Bill (*cutting cheese*) Your behaviour with that girl … (*He puts cheese on a plate*)

Sam Lewisham? She had spirit. I liked her. And so did you — if you were honest.

Bill I did not.

Sam You were dancing with her. Remember?

Bill It wasn't like that.

Sam It was! I was there. You were ecstatic!

Bill I was not.

Sam You were! You were! I saw you!

Bill (*sliding the plate with cheese on it in front of Sam*) Put the salad on there.

Sam prepares the salad during the following, Bill handing him items as he is asked for them

Sam D'you know, I still can't understand our Nan's reaction to your outrageous behaviour. Lettuce.

Bill It wasn't outrageous.

Sam She just laughed. Politely passed the time of day, and quietly took Lewisham back to the hotel.

Bill That's right.

Sam Not a harsh word. Tomatoes?

Bill We'll not see her again, I'm pleased to say.

Sam Lewisham will be back, you'll see. Coleslaw.

Bill She's ruined our game of Ludo. It's her turn.

Sam There you are! I told you, you'll miss her. Parsley.
Bill (*emphatically*) I will not miss her. We are not half-way through that game.
Sam And, of course, you were winning. Onion, I think. They're strong.
Bill That girl was running me a close second at Ludo. You were nowhere in it at all. A poor third.
Sam Ah, but don't forget that Lewisham beat you at draughts. Cucumber?
Bill Only with your help. She had no idea.
Sam Sour grapes?
Bill (*glancing at Sam*) We have no grapes.
Sam Sour grapes from you.
Bill No …
Sam That's finished. This is the best kitchen in town. (*He places the plates on a tray*) I'll take it in. (*He heads for the door*) You change the tape. The music's stopped.

Sam exits into the café

Bill stabs the order on hook five and then begins changing the tape

Linda enters the living-room from the street. She is wearing new clothes (traditional summer wear) and carries her old clothes in an untidy bundle. In her other hand she carries her holdall bag. She drops the bag and bundle on to the floor and moves into the kitchen

Linda Hi there, Bill.
Bill Oh! Oh, it's you.
Linda That's right — it's me.
Bill I — er — didn't recognize you, not at first.
Linda Have you missed me, then?
Bill (*unconvincingly*) Not really! It's your turn on the Ludo.
Linda You're not playing the same game?
Bill We've put a hold on it. Stuck the counters down with Blutack.
Linda Let me see that. (*She moves into the living-room*)
Bill (*following Linda*) We couldn't use the board so we played snakes and ladders last night. I won — three games to two.
Linda (*looking at the Ludo board*) Good for you.
Bill It's your turn. You were blue.
Linda I'm always bleedin' blue, me.
Bill We can abandon the game, if you're not stopping.
Linda Don't panic, Bill, I'm not stopping; only long enough to change these bloody silly clothes. (*She shakes the dice*) Three. (*She moves a counter*)

Sam enters the kitchen from the café

Sam Bill? Where are you? Two teas, table three: Glasgow, I suspect. (*He looks through the window into the café*) You should see table five tucking into the tuna flan.
Linda (*moving into the kitchen*) Hah! Hallo, Sam.

Bill follows Linda into the kitchen

Sam Lewisham! I knew you'd be back. (*To Bill*) Didn't I say?
Bill Yes, you did.
Sam (*examining Linda*) What's happened to your clothes?
Linda My old stuff is in the other room. Nan insisted on buying all this new. Isn't it terrible?
Sam No, it's very terrible, you're right. Did you sleep at the hotel?
Linda Yes.

Bill switches on the kettle

What did Nan have to say about us? Anything?
Linda Not a dicky bird. She's not interested in me this morning. Not sure why.
Bill Two teas? Is that all? (*He prepares the teapot during the following*)
Sam That's all.
Linda One of her friends has turned up from London. They've been in a huddle all morning giving it the chat. They shut up when I get near. They're coming here for tea later on.
Sam } (*together*) { What for?
Bill }   { Why is that?

Bill moves to the café window during the following

Linda I don't know, do I? Tea, they said. I shall be gone by then. They won't find me here. I'm definitely moving in with Vince today. Don't tell Nan, will you.
Sam No, no. Well …
Linda Promise?
Sam Promise.
Linda Can I use your phone? I want to ring him.
Sam Yes — if it's Arnold's lair you think you should fly.
Linda His name is Vince!
Sam He eats young ladies for breakfast.
Linda If he tries eating me he'll get indigestion, the sh … diarrhoea. (*She moves into the living-room, then returns*) By the way, you're honoured, I don't usually say diarrhoea. (*She moves back into the living-room*)

Bill (*at the café window*) Nan and her friend have just come in. See?

Sam (*moving to the window*) So they have.

Bill (*moving away*) Why are they here? That girl has to go.

Sam They're taking table one. They obviously want something to eat. You take their order.

Bill (*pouring tea*) No. Why me? You go.

Sam No.

Bill I'm making two teas.

Sam Shake you for it?

Bill (*after a hesitation*) All right.

Sam (*taking the dice from his pocket, shaking and throwing them*) Four and three — seven.

Bill (*collecting the dice*) Easy. (*He shakes and throws the dice*) Two ——

Sam And one. Three. You lose. (*He loads two teas on to the tray*)

Bill (*picking up the order pad*) I never win.

Sam You're unlucky, Bill. Very unlucky.

Bill picks up the tray and sulkily exits into the café

Sam fills the kettle, plugs it in and switches it on during the following. Linda dials a number on the telephone

Linda Hallo? ... I thought you were leaving yesterday? ... It doesn't matter who this is ... Who are you? ... What d'you mean — mind my own business? ... Because I'm moving in with Vince today. ... You've moved in today? Are you Hemel Hempstead?. ... What happened to her? ... Gone? I was to move in today. ... No, I am not the first reserve. (*She slams the phone down, moves to her bundle of clothes and begins to change*)

Bill enters excitedly from the café. He continues moving as he speaks

Bill (*in a loud whisper*) Sam! They're coming. They're coming. (*He keeps moving away*)

Sam Who?

Bill (*keeping his back to the café door*) Nan — and — the other person. They insist on coming out here. They're right behind me. See? They're behind ... They're looking for that girl.

Connie and Win enter, both with handbags. Win is obviously nervous

Sam closes the living-room door

Connie (*heartily*) Hallo, Mr Ellis!

Sam Oh, it's you.

Linda, partly dressed, crosses the living-room to listen at the door

Connie (*sardonically*) That's right. It's me — and this is my friend ——
Win Hallo.
Bill Oh!
Connie — and I've been telling her all about you two. Telling her how kind you've been to Linda?
Sam (*raising his voice*) If you're looking for Lewisham, she's not here.

Linda desperately gathers her clothes and bag, hurries up the stairs and exits

Win Lewisham?
Connie They call her Lewisham, our Linda, for some silly reason.
Win But that's where we live.
Connie We know that, dear. We know where we live. (*To Sam*) I'd like to introduce you to my friend. This is Mrs White.
Sam And I'm pleased to meet you, Mrs White.
Connie (*pointing her words*) This is — Mr Ellis?
Sam That's right, but call me Sam.
Connie Now I don't think we can do that. (*To Win*) Do you, dear? Much too personal, I think.
Win Yes, I think so.
Connie Too familiar by half. (*She turns to Bill*) And this is … D'you know, I don't think I know your name.
Bill Bill. It's Bill.

Bill and Sam exchange a look

Connie No, dear. I mean your surname.
Bill It really doesn't matter. Bill will do nicely. Thank you.
Connie Bill, I do believe you're trying to hide something from me.
Bill (*concerned*) No! No, nothing like that.
Connie Then what is your surname?
Bill (*concerned*) Oh. (*He panics*) It's — er — Ludo!
Connie Ludo?
Bill That's right. (*To Sam*) Isn't it?
Connie Mr Ludo?
Sam (*stepping in*) That is correct. Mr Ludo! (*Off the cuff*) We call him Mr Ludo — because that is — what he is — our champion Ludo player. We play Ludo all the time. Lewisham played it when she was here. The Ludo board is always in play, in the other room.
Bill Tiddly-winks as well … (*His voice fades away*)

Connie (*giving Bill a quizzical look*) Yes. Yes, I'd like to see the other room.
Sam (*anxiously*) Would you? (*He stands close to the door*)
Connie Yes. And I'm sure Mrs White would like to see the Ludo board.
Win No. I'm not bothered.
Connie Of course you're bothered, dear. Come along. (*To Sam*) Are you hiding anyone in there?
Sam (*raising his voice*) Now why should I be hiding anyone in there?
Connie No idea, except our Linda has disappeared.

Sam opens the door slowly and eases himself in. Bill screws up his face in anticipation

Sam (*relieved*) She's — er — um — she's not in here. There's no one here at all.
Bill (*surprised*) Isn't there?
Sam No.
Connie (*entering the living-room*) I did have the feeling she might be here. (*She moves to the Ludo board*)

Win follows Connie into the living-room and occasionally glances back at Bill who remains in the kitchen

Sam (*at the Ludo Board*) It's an old game. She was very fond of Ludo.
Connie Her name is Linda.
Sam She was blue. Bill is winning of course. That goes without saying: Mr Ludo. I'm green, and in my humble position: last.
Connie Ludo's a peculiar pastime for two grown men.
Sam Please, please! Ludo is not a pastime. It's a classical game, handed down from the Chinese — or was it the Egyptians?
Win (*moving in*) I thought it was Waddington's ... I used to play Ludo.
Sam Now there's a discerning lady.

Bill exits from the kitchen into the café

Connie I think, perhaps we should have some tea here, at this little table? You do do tea?
Sam Yes, we do do tea.
Win I enjoyed Ludo. Always did.
Connie Yes, dear. (*To Sam*) Tea for two and a selection of pastries. (*To Win*) Is that all right? (*She indicates the table*)

Win sits

Sam Tea for two and a selection of pastries – in here! (*He moves into the kitchen, closing the door behind him, and begins preparing the order*)

Connie (*earnestly*) There you are! Didn't I tell you? It's them! The pair of them! Well, isn't it?

Win Yes, it could be.

Connie Could be? It is them. Surely you recognized Arthur — or Bill, whatever he calls himself.

Win It's all like a dream to me.

Connie Hardly a bleedin' dream, dear. They're more like a pair of nightmares.

Win I didn't expect them to look like that.

Connie It's forty years on, Winifred. They begin to look like nightmares after forty years. Nightmares or prunes.

Win We're the same age as they are.

Connie We know that, dear — although they tell me I'm wearing very well.

Win (*surprised*) Do they really?

Connie Yes. And so are you, of course.

Win But those two haven't recognized us.

Connie Well, they wouldn't, would they? Men wouldn't. They're too stupid and selfish by half. Look at George. What a state he's in.

Win Your George looks more like your George than my Arthur looks like Arthur, if you know what I mean.

Connie No, I don't. What have those two old sods been doing all these years, I wonder.

Win (*concerned*) Connie, what are we going to do?

Connie One thing we must not do is mention our Christian names. If you call me "Connie" they will button on to that one. (*She stands*) What do they have here? (*She inspects details of the room during the following*)

Bill enters the kitchen from the café. He carries a tray

Bill What's happening? Where are they?

Sam (*indicating the living-room*) In there. Pot of tea and pastries, Mr Ludo.

Bill Well …

Sam Mr Ludo?

Bill I panicked, that's all. "Mr Ludo" just came out.

Sam We know that. I felt like giving you a good shake. Why didn't you say "Morgan"? That's the name you use.

Bill I don't like making up names.

Sam Blimey, Bill, it's for you we're doing it; using our real names only when we have to. You were the one who married again, not me.

Bill We can't be too careful.

Connie Can you believe they're living here together?

Win To be honest, I thought they were dead.

Connie There was a time when I hoped.

Bill I don't know why, but I feel very uneasy in their company. I shall be glad when they've gone and we can get back to how we were.

Connie And another thing. Have they ever married again? They could have deserted other women, after us.

Win I haven't considered that ...

Bill We shouldn't get involved. It's that girl's fault.

Bill and Sam continue working

Connie And another thing. Do they know we've divorced them? Um? Desertion?

Win How can I know what they know. We know so little.

Connie Then we must find out more.

Win If you want to know what I think — I think we should go home and leave things just as they are.

Connie No, we're here now. We'll have a little game with those two. They like playing games, do Mr Ellis and Mr Ludo. Do you know what I think? I think Fate has brought us here, and we must make the most of Fate's little smile.

Sam Here's the tea and pastries — done. Now you can take it in.

Bill Why me?

Sam Because it's your turn. I've had my throw. I took the order. It's your move now. I'll see how things are going on in here. (*He moves to the café door*)

Bill No, wait! I'll shake you for it.

Sam The dice? Bill, will you never learn? You're unlucky on the crunch games.

Sam exits into the café

Bill hesitates, then heads for the living-room

Connie I wonder how much those two are worth? Do they own this place, I wonder? You never know, we may be entitled, legally, to some of this.

Win I shouldn't think so.

Bill nervously enters the living-room

Connie Oh, there you are, Mr Ludo. Tea and pastries?

Bill No, it's Morgan.

Connie (*looking at the tray*) Tea and Morgan? Is it Welsh cakes?

Bill My name — it's Morgan. (*He begins unloading the tray. A rattling cup reveals his nervousness*)

Connie (*to Win*) Did you hear that, dear? Mr Ludo has suddenly become Mr Morgan — just like that — in the twinkling of an eye, or the tinkling of a tea cup. (*To Bill*) That's very nice china. You do things very well here, I must say.

Bill We do try.

Connie I gather from Linda, you've been doing this sort of thing for only two years.

Bill Yes, that's right — two years. (*During the following, he begins to realize who the two ladies are*)

Connie Well, fancy! (*To Win*) Did you hear that, dear? That's not long.

Win It's not long.

Connie And at their age. Your hand is shaking, Mr Ludo.

Bill Morgan.

Connie So what were you doing before this, Mr Ludo Morgan?

Bill (*concerned*) Before this?

Connie Yes, your work: and were you married?

Bill Oh! My work? Well, you know, just this and that, here and there, in and out — and ... (*He hesitates*)

Connie Now and then? You forgot now and then.

Bill (*finishing setting up the tea*) Yes, that's right. Now and then.

Connie Well, thank you for telling us all that — and so clearly.

Bill That's all right. Now, if you'll excuse me. There's work to be done. The café's getting very busy. (*He backs away*) Enjoy your pea and tastries — er — tea and pastries.

Connie Thank you. (*To Win*) Thank you dear?

Win Um? Oh, yes — thank you.

Bill hustles into the kitchen and thankfully closes the door behind him. He treads unsteadily to the work table, in a state of shock

Connie You see how cagey he was about the past? Did you notice? Shall I pour?

During the following Connie pours the tea and she and Win begin eating

Sam enters the kitchen from the café. During the following he sets to work to tidy up the kitchen

Sam It's getting busy in there. I've given a menu to table four. We have a tricky one there.

Bill (*vacantly*) What?

Sam Table four. Derbyshire, I think — or maybe Staffordshire. Somewhere north of Birmingham and south of Manchester. Mum, Dad, one child and Gran. (*He writes a note in his book*)

Bill Sam?

Sam Yes?

Bill You won't believe this. You won't. You won't believe what I'm going to say.

Sam Believe what?

Bill I know you won't. I can't believe it myself — yet.

Sam What's the matter. Believe what?

Bill (*swallowing hard*) Those two — those two women in there ... They ... they are Connie and Winifred.

Sam (*with amused incredulity*) Connie and Winifred?

Bill Shh! Yes.

Sam No! (*He moves away*) No! Don't be silly ... (*His voice fades*) My Connie and your ... ?

Bill It's them, I tell you. It's them!

Sam That's impossible.

Bill I don't think so.

Sam (*with forced confidence*) Well, there you are. It couldn't be them. (*He looks at the living-room door, then at Bill*) Could it?

Bill It could, and it is. Go in there and see for yourself.

Sam I will, I will. (*A short pause*) In a minute or two. I have to think — and there's work to do here.

Bill You're afraid.

Sam I am not afraid.

Bill Well, I am. I'm going into the café. (*He heads for the café*)

Sam You're a coward.

Bill Yes, I know that.

Bill exits into the café

Sam (*calling*) And it's not a café!

During the following, Sam continues tidying up, but with little concentration. His attention is regularly attracted to the living-room door

Win Are you sure it's my Arthur?

Connie Of course I'm sure you.

Win The thing is, it doesn't smell like my Arthur.

Connie Smell? What d'you mean, smell?

Win Arthur always had a smell about him. In fact I think I remember his smell better than I remember his face.

Connie What d'you mean? BO?

Win Oh, no! Nothing like that with Arthur.

Connie Smells don't last for forty years.

Win It was a mixture of cigarettes and Lifebuoy soap.

Connie He could have changed his smell by now, surely.

Win All the time we were married, he had the same smell.

Connie For three years?

Win (*reflectively*) Yes, that's all it was — three years.

Connie Three years is a long time for one smell to last.

Win D'you know, I don't think I really knew Arthur.

Connie I'd know George anywhere. Bastard. Have another cake.

Bill enters the kitchen from the café

Bill Have you been in there yet?

Sam No.

Bill What's happening?

Sam I've been thinking. When you say that's my Connie in there — and your Winifred ... Your Winifred was ... (*he thinks for a moment*) ... and ... D'you know, I can't remember clearly how she was — or Connie, if it comes to that. They were so young then.

Bill Well, go in there and take a good look at them now. Have a good look and listen.

Sam I'm going. I'm going.

Bill You're afraid.

Sam I'm not. I'm sure you're wrong. (*He moves to the living-room door*)

Bill Please God, let him be right, as he always is, and let me be wrong — as I always am.

Sam (*at the door*) Right. Here goes. (*He moves into the living-room, closing the door behind him*)

Bill moves cautiously to the door and listens

Sam Ah, there you are, ladies.

Connie Oh! Thought you'd forgotten us.

Sam Oh, no, no, no. Nothing like that. Is everything in order? (*He peers quizzically, though not obviously, at Connie and Win*)

Connie We were expecting a little more attention — Mr Ellis.

Sam Ah, yes! I'm sorry about that. We have been rather busy — er — Mrs —— ?

Connie Tozer.

Sam Ah — yes — Tozer — and Mrs — ?

Connie White.

Sam (*pondering*) That's right; it's Mrs Tozer and Mrs White.

Connie Is there something wrong, Mr Ellis?

Sam (*recovering*) No! No, there's nothing. As long as everything is in order here — the tea, the pastries — I'll leave you in peace. If you'll excuse me.

(*He makes a hurried exit into the kitchen*)

The door strikes Bill

Bill Ouch!!

Sam (*closing the door quickly*) What are you doing? (*Earnestly and with some anxiety*) It's them. You're right. I do believe it's them.

Bill I told you. Didn't I say?

Sam (*moving around*) I can't believe it. How has this happened? (*Not addressing Bill*) What's going on? (*He does not listen to Bill during the following*)

Bill (*following Sam*) I don't know.

Sam What are they doing here?

Bill I don't know.

Sam How did they get here?

Bill Don't know.

Sam Coincidence?

Bill Don't know.

Sam (*hearing Bill*) What?

Bill I said — I don't know.

Sam It couldn't be a coincidence, could it? No. Well, unlikely.

Bill Do they know who we are?

Sam They haven't got the faintest idea.

Bill But we know who they are. What makes you so sure?

Sam They are women, that's why. Too insensitive. Too credulous. I watched their faces. Not a glimmer of recognition. Typical!

Connie (*picking up the milk jug*) There's no milk left. That's typical. (*She stands up and moves towards the kitchen door, leaving her handbag*)

Bill What are we going to do?

Sam We must get rid of them — back to Lewisham!

Connie opens the door and enters the kitchen

Sam ⎱ (*together; startled*) ⎰ Ah!
Bill ⎰   ⎱ Oh!

Connie So there you are. We would like more milk — if it's no trouble.

Sam ⎱ (*together*) ⎰ Yes, of course.
Bill ⎰   ⎱ Yes, yes.

Sam and Bill step forward and collide

Sam No trouble, I'll do it.

Bill I can do it.

Sam (*taking the jug*) No, it's me. (*During the following he fills the jug with milk*)

Connie (*moving around the kitchen*) Dear, dear, dear. No fighting, please. I must say, this is a very pleasant little kitchen. (*To Sam*) I do know about these things. I keep a pub. I do bar food and light snacks — just as you do.

Win moves from the living-room table to the threshold of the kitchen

Sam (*indignantly*) We do not do bar food and light snacks. We are purveyors of wholesome, homemade, light but good food.

Bill's state of nervousness forces him to speak. He addresses himself, more than Connie, during the following

Bill (*a mumbling echo*) Wholesome, homemade, light but good food …
Connie It's the same thing.
Bill The same thing.
Sam It's not the same thing.
Bill No, it's not the same …
Sam It's an entirely different cuisine.
Connie Oh, my God! Listen to that! Who do you think you are? It's a little café you have here, that's all.
Sam It's not a café.
Bill (*mumbling*) It's not a café.
Connie What is it then?
Sam I don't know. I haven't found a suitable word for it — yet. It's above being a café, but not quite a restaurant. There is a word, I'm sure. (*He absent-mindedly puts the milk in the microwave during the following*)
Bill (*anxiety speaking*) A caférant.
Sam (*to Bill*) What are you talking about?
Bill (*fading*) I don't know … (*He sees what Sam is doing with the milk*) Don't put that in there!

Sam takes the milk out of the microwave

Connie (*to Sam*) I understand, Mr Ellis, you've been at this little café game for a very short time. What were you doing before this?
Sam I was filling a jug with milk.
Connie Very funny. You must have been in some sort of trade. Or is there something in your past you're trying to hide?
Sam No, nothing like that.
Connie Well, then, what were you doing?
Sam Doing? (*Pause*) Well — I — er — travelled a bit. Moved around. Used the feet. (*Inspired*) Yes, I used the feet. I was a chiropodist.

Win Well, I never … (*She moves into the room*)
Connie You must be joking! You were never a chiropodist.
Sam How d'you know that? You know nothing about me. (*Pause*) Do you?

Linda enters and descends the staircase, stopping half-way down

There is a pause

Connie (*backing down*) No. No, I don't.
Win (*to Sam, simply*) Then you must know Mr Wainwright, Sam. Wainwright.

This cuts across the conversation. There is a sudden silence

He's a chiropodist.

Linda completes her descent of the stairs and listens to the following from the living-room

Connie For God's sake.
Win (*to Bill*) I see Mr Wainwright every week — with my feet. I have two bunions.
Bill Really?
Win One on each foot.
Bill That's very unusual.
Win Is it?
Bill I think so. Bunions are very unpleasant — especially two at a time.
Connie Forget your damned feet, Winifred.
Win Connie!

Linda moves quickly into the kitchen

Linda (*angrily*) Cor blimey! Why don't you four silly sods get sorted? Right? (*To Connie*) You know who these two are! I've been listening. (*To Sam*) And I'm guessing you know who they are! Sort yourselves out for God's sake. And who's looking after the café? Nobody! Right? Don't bother. I'll do it. (*She moves towards the café door and stops*) OK, Sam! I know! It's not a café!

Linda exits into the café

There is a tense pause

Connie George.
Sam Connie.

Win Arthur.
Bill Winifred.

C<small>URTAIN</small>

ACT II
Scene 1

The same. Only seconds later than the end of Act I

The Curtain *rises*

Connie And so, it's Arthur.
Bill (*mixing the words with an uncomfortable cough*) Yes — that's right.
Sam And Winifred?
Win Yes, George?
Sam No, I was just saying: it's you.
Win Oh! Yes — it's me.

A short pause

Sam (*lightly*) Well, well, well!
Connie Well, well, well? Is that all you have to say?
Sam What else is there to say?
Connie I would have thought there was more than enough to say, George
  Wilkins. That's your name, George Wilkins; and he is Arthur Wilkins and
  don't forget it. George and Arthur Wilkins, not Bill and bleedin' Ben. You
  both have a lot of things to answer for.
Sam Now why d'you say that?
Connie Why do I … ? Because you two walked out on us — her and me —
  nearly forty years ago, and we haven't seen a hair or hide of you since.
Sam Now that's not true. I left you a note.
Connie A note? It was a scrappy piece of paper saying "See you soon —
  George." You call that a note?
Sam Well, it was sort of prophetic.
Connie Prophetic?
Sam Hasn't it come true? I have seen you — today.
Connie You said soon. D'you call forty years on soon?
Sam That's not very soon, no.

*Linda enters from the café. She carries a tray, on which are two empty
sugar pots and a few items of crockery. She has an order with her too*

Linda Will you keep your noise down? The customers will hear you.

Win (*gently to Bill*) You didn't leave me a note.
Bill No. No, I didn't.
Win I wondered — that's all.
Linda Two apple pie and cream. One strawberry ice-cream and one cheesecake — blackcurrant. Table three. (*She stabs the slip on hook three*) Table four have gone. They're fed up waiting.

Sam and Bill welcome the distraction

Sam (*eagerly*) I'll do the apple pie.
Bill No, I can do that.
Sam You do the cheesecake.
Bill Oh, yes — the cheesecake. Right.
Linda Blackcurrant.
Bill I'll do that.
Sam And the strawberry ice is mine as well. Excuse me. (*He eases past Connie, goes to the board and confirms the order*) Excuse me.

From now on, as lunchtime approaches, Connie and Win find themselves in the flow and hustle of the preparation of the food. Connie is determined to keep the conversation going, but has to compete with the physical countermoves and the verbal counterpoint of the kitchen. Sam and Bill use the activity as a form of protection

Linda The café's filling up and table five want their bill.
Bill (*eagerly*) Shall I do that?
Linda No, I'll do that. You can fill these sugar pots. They're empty.
Bill Yes, I can do that. Right.

Linda places the sugar pots on a work surface and continues to the sink with the tray. Connie follows Linda, aggressively. This action frightens Bill away from the sugar pots

Connie (*to Linda*) You've changed your clothes?
Linda (*discarding a few items from the tray*) So I have. So what?

Sam crosses to the fridge and takes out an apple pie

Sam Is the apple pie hot or cold?
Linda Hot.
Connie Listen … .
Sam You must write the information down – hot or cold.
Connie (*to Linda*) What's happened to the clothes I bought you?

Linda (*crossing to the order board*) I'm going to throw them in the sea, when the tide comes in.

Connie You cheeky little cow!

Linda Oh, charming! Moo, moo! Excuse me. (*She takes the bill from the hook and pushes past Connie*)

Connie I'm talking to you.

Linda (*ignoring Connie*) I've taken the bill — table five?

Sam Good.

Linda exits into the café. Sam carries the apple pie to a work surface. Bill hovers

Connie So, then, what happened to you?

Sam (*innocently*) Me? I haven't been anywhere, as far as I know. I've been here all the time …

Connie Now don't be funny with me, George Wilkins. You know very well what I mean.

Bill crosses carefully to the fridge to remove the cheesecake; he looks into the fridge with his head almost in it

Sam Oh — you mean … Where was I …

Connie That's exactly what I mean.

Sam Well, it was a long time ago. Times now long past. (*He moves past Bill and heads for the plate store*)

Connie I know that. You don't have to tell me it was a long time ago.

Sam And I agree, it was. Wasn't it Bill?

Bill (*lifting his head*) Pardon?

Sam A long time ago.

Bill Oh yes, it was.

Sam (*collecting two plates and returning to the work surface with them*) Looking for the cheesecake?

Bill That's right.

Sam places the plates on the work surface and cuts the apple pie during the following, placing two pieces on plates

Connie (*to Sam*) It may have been a long time ago, but I remember it well, oh yes. Shall I remind you? We were married for three years, that's all: three years and you disappeared.

Bill finds the cheesecake and takes it to a work surface

Sam Correction. (*He takes the two plates of apple pie to the microwave*) I
  didn't disappear. I did move on, yes, but I did remain visible.
Connie Now don't try playing the fool with me.
Sam Delightful apple pie. Home made.

During the following, Bill cuts the cheesecake, trying to keep a low profile.
Win hovers close to the living-room door

Connie (*firmly*) So what happened to you?
Sam Me? Nothing …
Connie What d'you mean — nothing?
Sam Nothing very much — not at first. I caught a train to Folkestone.
Connie (*momentarily thrown*) Folkestone?
Sam That's right.
Connie Was there another woman?
Sam (*after a pause*) No, there wasn't another woman.
Connie Yes, you were no capture, that's for sure. You were nobody. Nobody
  of any consequence. Although, there were one or two thought the sun
  shone from your backside. God knows why. And don't imagine I didn't
  know what was going on, either. Gracie Brookfield, for one.
Sam (*putting the plates of apple pie in the microwave*) Gracie Brookfield?
Connie You remember Gracie Brookfield. Red hair from the bottle and tight
  green dresses.
Bill Racey Gracie!
Sam (*setting the microwave timer*) Oh, her! Fifty seconds. (*He moves away*)
Connie Yes, her. She always had a soft spot for you — and we all know
  where that was. (*To Win*) Win, you remember her.
Win (*timidly*) Yes. Yes, I do.

Bill reacts to Win's voice

Connie It was a humiliating time for me. I never left the flat for three weeks.
Sam (*to Bill*) Cream?
Connie What?
Sam I said — cream. (*To Bill*) We shall want the cream. (*He moves to the
  fridge*)
Bill Yes, we will.
Connie (*to Bill*) And what about you then, Arthur?
Bill Pardon?
Connie Was it all planned? You two off together?
Sam (*taking the cream jug from the fridge*) Nothing planned at all.

Linda enters from the café, holding an order

Linda Two quiche salads — table two. (*She stabs the order on hook two*)

Sam Two quiche salads. Give me the cheesecake, Bill.

Connie (*to Win*) Winifred, don't just stand there. Sort something out with Arthur.

Win I'm all right here.

Connie draws Win into the kitchen during the following

Bill (*anxiously*) Yes; I'm all right too. (*He takes the jug from Sam*) The cream. I'm all right. I'm pouring the cream. See. (*He pours cream on the cheesecake*)

Linda Don't forget the sugar pots want filling.

Linda exits into the café

The microwave timer "pings"

Sam Apple pie's done. (*During the following he removes the two dishes of apple pie from the microwave*)

Connie Say something, Winifred.

Win (*to Connie; nervously*) Yes — yes. I saw Gracie Brookfield recently. She weighs fifteen stone.

Sam ⎱
Bill ⎰ (*together*) Fifteen stone?

Connie Not that. We want to know why these two went off together.

Win (*unconvincingly*) Yes, that's what we'd like to know.

Sam I didn't go off with Gracie Brookfield.

Connie I know that. You went off with him.

Sam I did not. He left three months after me. I was in Paris by that time.

Connie Paris? You?

Bill returns the cream jug to the fridge and takes out a container of ice-cream

Bill I'll do the ice-cream. (*He prepares the ice-cream serving during the following*)

Connie I don't believe that. Do you, Win? Paris?

Win I don't know.

Connie Of course we don't believe it. (*To Sam*) You could never speak French. You could never speak English properly — not you.

Win eases herself into the living-room and sits down during the following

Sam But I could repair boats. D'you remember that?

Connie Boats?
Sam Where's the cream?
Connie What?
Bill In the fridge.
Connie You were a carpenter, I remember. That's what you were.
Sam Right. Chatham dockyard. Ships, boats — whatever.
Connie And there are no ships in Paris. I'm not daft. You're a liar, George.
You always were.
Sam That's not fair. And there are boats in Paris — small ones. I met this chap
in a pub in Folkestone. He was looking for a carpenter shipwright. He had
a small boatyard in Argentuil.
Connie Where?
Sam Argentuil. It's on the Seine — near Paris. But you know that, I'm sure.
(*He takes the cream from the fridge and pours some on the portions of pie
during the following*)
Connie I bloody well don't know that.
Sam Oh! I worked there for two years, and then I went to the south of France
for a year or so, and then on, over the hills and far away. Small boats opened
up the world for me.
Connie The world? Hah?
Sam (*placing the jug on the surface*) That's right. Florida, Jacksonville and
the St John's River, South America, Maldives, the Philippines …
Connie Working on boats.
Sam Small boats. There's earnings to be made in small boats — around the
world.

*Bill completes the ice-cream order and returns the container to the fridge
with the cream jug*

Two plates for quiche salad. (*He collects two plates from the plate store*)

Linda enters from the café with an order and a bill

Linda Two ploughman's with jock egg, two teas — table one. We're getting
busy. (*She stabs the order on hook one*)
Bill (*confirming the order*) Two ploughman's with Scotch egg, two teas —
table one. (*To Connie*) And we're getting busy.
Linda And I'm having trouble with this guy on table five. He says I've added
the bill up wrong.
Bill (*eagerly*) Let me see it.

Bill takes the bill from Linda

Linda All right — don't snatch.

Bill I'll see to it.

Bill exits into the café

Sam (*to Linda*) Order ready — table three. Two apple pie with cream, one cheesecake, one ice-cream. On your way. (*He takes a quiche from the fridge*)
Linda Yes, sir! (*She picks up the tray*) At once. (*She moves away*) It's all go, go, go.

Linda exits into the café

Connie That's a nice-looking quiche. Did you buy it in?
Sam Certainly not! I made it. We make everything here — if it's possible. We buy very little in. (*He cuts two slices of quiche during the following*)
Connie (*turning to the living-room door*) Did you hear that, Win? Winifred, where are you? (*She moves to the living-room door*) Win? Are you hiding in there again? (*She enters the living-room*) Would you believe they make their own quiche?
Win No, I wouldn't … .
Connie He says they make everything. Now why don't you go in there and find out more about Arthur — and what he's been up to.
Win I don't think I want to do that.
Connie Nonsense. I intend getting to the bottom of everything here — oh yes. Did you hear him? George? While I've been slogging away all my life, he's been flaunting himself around the world as he pleases.
Win It doesn't matter now, surely.
Connie It does matter. Come along! Why should I have had all the suffering and he all the pleasure.

Connie eases Win from her chair

I'll make him pay.
Win You haven't suffered all that much.
Connie (*crossing to the kitchen door*) Oh, but I have, Win, I have.

Connie leads Win into the kitchen

Now George, here is Winifred. (*To Win*) Say something to George. You must have something to say to him.

Win and Sam exchange and hold a meaningful look for a few seconds

Win Are you keeping well, George?

Sam Yes. And you, Winifred?

Win Yes.

Sam Good.

Win Yes — good.

Sam More lettuce, I think. (*He goes to fridge and takes some lettuce from it*)

Connie Is that all?

Sam Yes, but we've got more lettuce in the fridge.

Connie (*to Win*) I meant, is that all she can say? After all, you are her brother-in-law.

Sam Was. Was her brother-in-law.

Connie Why d'you say that?

Sam You've married again ... I think?

Connie (*glancing at Win*) Who said so?

Sam Nobody said so. You've changed your names. (*He returns to the work surface with the lettuce, puts the lettuce with the quiche and adds other salad items*)

Connie That means nothing. A person can change their names. You for one ——

Bill enters from the café

Bill (*to himself*) That's sorted out.

Connie (*to Bill*) — and him, for another.

Bill Me? (*To Sam*) Oh — er — table two are enquiring ... .

Sam Table two is ready. Two quiche salads. (*He moves to the order board*) Two teas later on, tell them. (*He looks at the order on hook one*) Two ploughman's next — take one.

Bill begins loading a tray

Connie There he is then, Win. There's Arthur.

Win Yes, I know that.

Sam Is this ploughman a Cheddar, Stilton or what?

Bill I don't know.

Sam She hasn't written it down. (*He collects some plates*) Cheddar's favourite.

Connie Well, say something.

Win Yes, I will. (*To Bill*) You're very busy.

Connie Not that kind of question, stupid.

Bill But I am. She's quite right — we are busy. (*He lifts the tray*) Very busy indeed. You don't know. Excuse me. (*He heads for the café door*)

Linda bursts through the café door carrying a tray of used crockery and cutlery

Linda and Bill both swerve skilfully but fail to avoid a glancing blow. Bill's tray maintains equilibrium but Linda's tray crashes to the floor

Linda Bill, look where you're going!

Bill exits into the café

Sam There is absolutely no excuse for that behaviour.
Connie (*with false concern*) Dear, oh dear, oh dear, oh dear.
Win (*to Sam*) Can I help?
Connie You stay just where you are, Winifred.
Linda (*to Connie, angrily*) Are you still here?
Connie Yes, I'm still here.
Linda Thought you'd be gone by now. You're bugging the place — d'you know that? (*To Sam*) Where's the pan and brush? Oh, I know.
Sam I'll do it. I'll do it. (*He collects a brush and pan during the following*)
Linda (*to Connie*) Now let's get it sorted. I'm not going back to London, I tell you, with you or anybody else. Right?
Connie Please yourself dear. I'm not bothered. What are you going to do? Stay here with those two?
Linda No, I've done my own arrangements. (*A sudden thought*) Oh, I forgot: two specials with jacket spuds. (*She produces an order and stabs it on hook six*) Table six.

Bill enters from the café

Sam Two tuna flan! Now there's a discerning customer.
Bill Is it all right now? I'll fill the sugar pots.

Linda takes the brush and pan from Sam

Linda I'll do it. You'll do your back in. (*She kneels and begins clearing up. To Connie*) It's embarrassing, you turning up like this. It really is.

Sam washes his hands and returns to preparing the ploughman's lunch

Connie Oh, yes. It's embarrassing for a lot of people. And I'm not leaving here until a certain person decides to tell me why he cleared off and left me.
Sam (*quietly*) Onions?
Connie What?
Sam Pickled onions.
Bill (*to Linda*) Where are the sugar pots?
Connie (*to Sam*) I'm waiting for an answer.
Bill (*to Connie*) No. I was asking her. (*He indicates Linda*)

Linda (*to Bill*) They're over here.
Bill Oh. (*He collects the sugar pots during the following*)
Sam (*to Connie*) Would you really like to know?
Bill (*passing*) Pardon?
Sam Not you.
Bill Sorry.
Connie (*to Sam*) Yes, I would like to know. That's why I'm standing here — waiting.
Linda (*on her knees*) And you're standing in my way, if you don't mind. I'm trying to clear this up.

Connie moves away. Movement in the kitchen has become more difficult. Connie, Win and Linda have all to be negotiated by Sam and Bill

Bill (*passing between Sam and Connie with the sugar pots, talking more to himself*) Sugar pots haven't been filled. People are waiting for them.
Sam (*to Connie*) All right. I'll tell you.
Bill Pardon?
Sam Not you.
Bill Sorry. (*He reaches the cupboard, takes out a jar and fills the sugar pots during the following*)
Sam (*to Connie*) I'll tell you — if you really want to know. (*A short pause*) I think it was all a mistake. Scotch eggs. (*He eases past Connie to get the Scotch eggs*)
Connie What d'you mean — mistake?
Sam Me marrying you ——
Connie Oh, really!
Sam — at the time. And a mistake for you, I might add, at the time.
Connie And you could be right there. But I'll decide when I make a mistake, if you don't mind.
Sam I don't mind at all. (*He moves away*) But you said it just a short while ago, as a matter of fact.
Connie Said what?

Linda hits Sam with the brush

Win eases her way back to the living-room and sits during the following

Sam (*to Linda*) Come along! Are you getting it cleared up?
Linda I've done it. (*She stands up*)
Sam Two teas — table one.
Linda I'll do that. (*She makes two teas during the following*)
Connie So what did I say, just now?

Sam What? Ah, yes. You said I was a nobody.

Connie And you were, that's right — a nobody.

Sam Nobody of any consequence. You said that.

Connie That's right — you were.

Sam And that's how I saw it at the time — exactly. Two ploughman's with Scotch egg — nearly finished. And d'you know when I decided to change all that, being a nobody? I'll tell you. It was one night at the cinema. The Odeon, if I remember correctly. D'you remember the Odeon? On the corner of ——

Connie I remember the Odeon ... .

Sam (*to Linda*) Is that mess cleared up?

Linda Yes.

Sam It wants the sweeper on it now.

Linda I'm doing the teas.

Sam Two tuna flan specials next.

Bill (*crossing the room, mumbling*) Fish pie ...

Sam It's not fish pie.

Bill Sorry.

Sam Got to get the carpet sweeper. (*He moves into the living-room*)

Win stands up

Don't stand up for me, Winifred. Just passing through.

Connie (*following Sam into the living-room*) So what about the Odeon? I remember the Odeon.

Sam Ah, yes, the Odeon. That was a vital evening for me. I was there with you. (*He picks up the carpet sweeper*) It was a Humphrey Bogart film. Can't for the life of me remember which one. Handy little things, these sweepers.

Connie Humphrey Bogart?

Sam Yes. I was watching Bogie in the film, and what he was up to, and it struck me, there and then, quite suddenly — (*he heads for the kitchen*) — how much he was like me ——

Connie What?

Sam and Connie enter the kitchen

Sam — or how I wanted to be. His style of living was much more interesting.

Linda I'm on my way.

Linda exits into the café with the tray

Connie (*incredulously*) What are you talking about, George? The film?

Sam Yes, the film. Bogart got around, meeting interesting people and doing interesting things, in cars, taxis, aeroplanes. There was always room for him at the bar — and the barman would be there waiting. A taxi was always passing when he wanted one. When he parked his car there was always a space.

Connie You're talking about a film.

Sam When he was with Lauren Bacall, he never wanted a jimmy riddle.

Connie That's not real life, is it? Blimey, we all wanted to be like they were in the films.

Sam But who tried it? I did. Travelled the world, in my own film.

Connie (*amused*) Being like Humphrey Bogart?

Sam Yes, in spirit.

Connie Well, Bogart wouldn't use a carpet sweeper on floor tiles, would he. He was too smart for that.

Sam looks at the sweeper and puts it to one side

Linda enters carrying an empty vinegar bottle

Linda Has anyone got a pencil? I've broken m' pencil.

Bill Here's one. (*He hands Linda a pencil*)

Linda Thanks. This vinegar bottle needs filling.

Sam Take a fresh one. Over there.

Bill I'll do it. (*He picks up a full bottle of vinegar*)

Linda Are you doing nothing in here?

Linda puts down her bottle and exits into the café

Sam (*calling*) Yes, and we're busy doing it.

Bill I have the vinegar. (*He heads for the café door*)

Sam On your way then, Bill.

Bill exits into the café

Connie His name is Arthur.

Bill enters

Bill Yes? ... Oh.

Bill exits into the café

Sam (*moving to the order board*) Now then — what next? Table six?

Connie George, you had to go at some time.

Sam What?

Connie You had to have a jimmy riddle at some time.

Sam Well, you have to, don't you. But not Bogie. He must have taken tablets.

Connie You're a bloody dreamer, George, a dreamer.

Sam I know ... (*He collects the tuna flan from the fridge*)

Connie Dreamers achieve nothing. D'you know that?

Sam Maybe.

Connie And I don't believe a word of that Humphrey Bogart story rubbish. Not a word of it.

Sam Of course you don't. That's because you're not a dreamer, Connie. You never were.

Sam prepares two tuna flan salads with jacket potatoes during the following

Connie (*moving to the living-room door*) Winifred, did you hear any of that?

Win Yes. Yes, I heard some of it. It was George speaking.

Connie (*moving into the living-room*) I know it was George speaking. Did you hear him say he was Humphrey Bogart?

Win He looks nothing like Humphrey Bogart.

Connie We know that, Winifred ... .

Win Well, just a little bit, maybe, about the eyes — otherwise, nothing like.

Bill enters from the café

Bill (*to Sam*) Where are they? Are they gone?

Sam They're in there. (*He indicates the living-room and continues working*)

Bill clears and washes up during the following

Win (*to Connie*) When are we going back to London?

Connie When we've finished our business here, that's when.

Win Connie, why don't you give up? You married Dermot, remember.

Connie Don't you mention Dermot's name here. Not here. Are you not interested in what happened to Arthur? You should be.

Win He's still very light on his feet. He moves well. He was a dancer, you know.

Connie Yes, I remember that. And no good can come of marrying a man who earns his living with his feet.

Win (*considering*) Oh, I don't know. Mr Wainwright does.

Connie Who?

Win Mr Wainwright — my chiropodist.

Connie Oh, him. Well, it's not *his* feet is it. It's with other people's feet he earns his living. That's another sort I could never take a liking to — a man who pokes and picks at other people's feet.

Win He's very particular regarding hygiene.

Bill What are we going to do about them — in there?

Sam Keep our heads, that's what we're going to do, keep our heads. Those with the strongest nerve win the game.

Bill It's not a game.

Sam It's a game. Everything's a game.

Bill It's all right for you. You didn't marry again.

Sam You could be saved yet. They've changed their names, remember, which means they married again. They're denying it — but they could be bluffing.

Connie I see Arthur is in there again.

Connie eases Win from the living-room towards the kitchen during the following

For God's sake come and have a word with him.

Win I've had a word with him.

Connie Surely you'd like to know what he's been up to all this time?

Win No, I don't think so.

Connie and Win reach the threshold of the kitchen

Connie So there you are again, Arthur. Winifred has something to say.

Win Well … I don't know …

Bill Has she?

Connie Yes. (*A short pause*) Winifred?

Win (*after a pause in which she winds herself up*) Yes. (*Short pause*) There is something I'd like to know.

Connie Good. So what would you like to know then, Winifred?

Win (*tensely*) It's just that if Arthur and George didn't leave together, how did they get together now?

Connie My! Yes! That's a good question, Winifred. You've been listening. What about that one, Arthur? (*She indicates Sam*) If that one there was touring the world as Humphrey Bogart, how did you manage to meet again?

Bill He found me.

Connie Found you? Were you lost?

Bill No.

Sam No. (*Lightly*) I had a sudden compulsion to return to England. Curious, that, after travelling the world for most of my life. So, I came back, drifted up to Camden, looking for some of the old haunts, and met a guy who knew where Bill was working — so I went to ——

Linda enters carrying a tray and an order

Linda Two coffees, one orange squash — table five. (*She puts the order on hook five*)
Bill I'll do that. (*He prepares coffee during the following*)
Linda I'll do the orange squash. The little kid's in there sniffling and whining. (*She prepares a glass of squash*)
Connie (*to Sam*) So where did you find him?
Linda On table five.
Connie Not you. Him. Where were you working?
Sam Me?
Connie Not you. Him. Where was he working?
Sam I found him on the Isle of Man.
Connie The Isle of Man? Arthur? (*To Bill*) What were you doing on the Isle of Man?
Bill I — er — I was a bingo caller.
Win (*with sudden interest*) Oh, really ... !
Connie (*to Bill*) What did you say?
Win (*helpfully*) He said he was a bingo caller.

Linda exits into the café with the orange squash

Connie I heard what he said ... .
Win (*to Bill*) I go to bingo, once a week.
Connie Bingo caller? You? That's not a proper job, bingo calling.
Sam A nice little number, bingo calling. Right, Bill?
Bill That's right! If you're a bingo caller — your days are numbered!
Connie And your days will be bloody numbered if you keep on. I don't believe a word of it. It's all a pack of lies. You've called this café of yours by the right name: "Cobblers". Cobblers is the right name for it. That's what you talk, the pair of you, a load of old cobblers.
Sam We called it "Cobblers", because of the street outside; it's cobbled.
Connie And "cobblers" to that as well!

Linda enters from the café

Linda Can we have a little less "girls and boys" in here? They can hear you out there. Table six are grumbling. They want their tuna flan. And there's a guy in there with a party of fourteen.
Sam Fourteen? (*He looks through the window into the café*)
Linda Fourteen little kids he says. A Boy Scouts cricket team in a mini-bus.
Sam We don't take coach parties. Tell him — no.
Linda They are just little kids.
Sam I don't care.
Linda Right — I'll tell him.
Sam Take the table six order. It's finished. Two specials with jackets.

Linda picks up the tray and exits into the café

Bill (*anxious to escape*) I'll follow. I'll take the two coffees. I'm following her.

Bill exits into the café carrying the two coffees

Connie (*to Sam*) I can't understand that. You turning down trade — like fourteen punters all at the same time.

Sam Well, I'm fussy about the type of customer we have here.

Connie Fussy? You'll never make money at this game being fussy.

Sam That's my business. I'm not in it to make a lot of money.

Connie Then why are you doing it?

Sam For fun. A game, that's all. A pastime.

Connie At your age — why?

Sam To avoid the thoughts of dying for one thing. And I like meeting people. A café is a place for meeting people without getting too involved. People come and go: "Hallo", "Goodbye". I like that.

Connie So you don't like getting involved with people.

Sam Not permanently. Just keep moving on.

Connie Then I feel sorry for you, George.

Sam Oh, please don't feel sorry for me. I'm perfectly happy. And another thing — Bill has received a steady little income. He was in a bad state, financially, when I found him.

Connie Then Arthur doesn't own any of this.

Sam No. It belongs to me.

Connie (*changing the mood*) So then, George, you must have some money tucked away somewhere, if this is all for fun?

Sam Oh no, I wouldn't say that.

Bill enters with an order

Bill Two soups, two rolls and butter, two chicken salad — table seven. (*He puts the order on hook seven and prepares the meals during the following*)

Sam (*to Connie*) Is there anything we can get you? A pot of tea, in the living-room?

Connie You won't get rid of us that easy. (*To Bill*) So then, Arthur, did you ever marry again?

Bill (*with signs of panic*) What?

Connie You heard what I said.

Bill Me? (*His voice croaks and he coughs*) Me?

Connie Yes, you. Winnie would like to know.

Bill No. No, I'm not married. Not married at all.

Connie Then he could still be married to Winifred. And you could still be married to me.

Sam No. No, I don't think so.

Bill (*echoing Connie*) I don't think so … .

Connie Both of you could have legal responsibilities to us.

Sam Oh, no. Not if you married again.

Connie You keep saying that, George. Who said we married again?

Sam There's Lewisham — for one.

Connie Linda? What about Linda?

Sam She's your grandchild. To have grandchildren, you have children first.

Connie I had a child, yes, a daughter. What's that to do with marriage?

Linda enters from the café

Linda One gâteau and one carrot cake — table one. (*She stabs the order on the board*) They're in a hurry.

Sam One gâteau and one carrot cake. We're getting behind with orders. This kitchen's going to pot.

Linda Well, it's all this bloody chat going on out here.

Connie It's family matters chat, my girl.

Linda And some family ours is. My parents cleared off when I was a kid, and now it looks like a long lost grandfather has turned up.

Connie He's not your grandfather. (*To Sam*) I can sue you — d'you know that? — for desertion.

Sam Not if you married again.

Connie Who said I married again?

Linda Oh! Then if you didn't marry that bloody old Irish drunk, Dermot, does that mean I'm a grand bastard?

Connie Shut up! You know nothing about it.

Linda Now that's true. I know nothing. (*To Sam*) And Sam, you can't ask poor old Dermot; he died a few years ago, suffering from a dose of Irish whiskey saturation.

Connie Will you shut up!

Bill (*at the café window*) Be quiet. The customers will be complaining!

Sam (*banging a tray on a surface*) Well let them! Let them! I don't care! I'm finished. I'm finished for the day!

Bill But it's only lunchtime.

Sam I don't care! I really don't care! (*To Bill, deliberately*) If she wants to come in here pushing us around, and around … We were perfectly happy here, you and me, perfectly happy. I don't know what her game is. If she's got some kind of plan … OK! I concede the game. (*He throws a metal tray to the floor*) I don't care. In fact, I couldn't care less. I'm going out. (*He moves into the living-room*)

Connie You're a coward.

Sam That's right. I am!

Connie Running away again.

Sam (*opening the street door*) Running away again — and again, and again, if I have to.

Connie (*derisively*) Is it Humphrey Bogart again?

Sam Yes! And here's looking at you, kid!

Sam exits, slamming the door

Connie (*shouting*) Play it again, Sam!!

Win moves slowly into the living-room. She and Connie stand looking at the street door

Linda and Bill remain in the kitchen; they begin working

Win (*to Connie*) You should have told him we both married again. That wasn't fair.

Connie (*calmly*) Nothing's fair, Winifred. Nothing ever is fair.

CURTAIN

SCENE 2

The same. Thirty minutes later

There is an order on hook one

Connie has now taken over in the kitchen. She is wearing a striped apron and is busily preparing salad. In the living-room, Bill and Win are sitting motionless at each end of the table, facing DS

Linda enters the kitchen from the café and stabs an order on a hook

Linda How are things going on in here? Coping?

Connie Course I'm coping! I'm not a learner. I'm used to this sort of thing.

Linda (*looking through the window to the café*) It's easing off a bit in there. Not many people now.

Connie One ham salad with Scotch egg, and one quiche on its own. I'm doing the salad.

Linda Shall I do the quiche?

Connie It's about time you did something.

Linda What d'you mean? I've been working like a donkey, in and out of that café like a bleedin' trombone.
Connie I'm wondering why we're bothering at all.
Linda Because we can't let people down. If you hadn't turned up in the first place, everything would have been all right.
Connie And if you hadn't been here in the first place, I wouldn't have turned up at all. Right?
Linda Right! It's a cock-up all round.
Connie That's right. A cock-up!
Linda All round!
Connie All round!

Connie continues with the salad and Linda cuts a slice of quiche during the following; when ready, they put the meals on a tray

Where d'you think George has gone?
Linda George? In the pub, I reckon. The *Sailors Arms* — that's where he'd go to sulk. And he won't be back till you've gone. (*Short pause*) I like Sam.
Connie George.
Linda He could have been my grandad.
Connie But he isn't. What about Arthur?
Linda Oh, he's all right, in a funny sort of way. (*She looks at the living-room door*) Are those two still in there? I don't think they've said a word.
Connie Not surprised.
Linda I'll see what's going on. (*She moves to the living-room door and listens*) It's very quiet. Perhaps they've gone and died.
Connie Don't be stupid.
Linda Well, they could have killed each other in some sort of crime of passion.
Connie Very unlikely. They were always like that — quiet. I blame her. He went into his shell because of her. She changed him completely.
Linda And why did Sam leave you?
Connie That's none of your business. The salad is ready.
Linda Good. The quiche is done.
Connie I'll take them in, if you're feeling like a donkey with a trombone.
Linda No, I'll do it. It's getting quiet. Put your feet up and give the old skittles an interval. (*She picks up the tray*) That's an order for leg rest.
Connie There's nothing wrong with my legs.
Linda (*heading for the café door*) Don't knock old legs. Old legs can knock on their own. That's one of Sam's sayings.
Connie (*thoughtfully*) Yes, I can imagine. (*Short pause*) I think I'll go for a walk.
Linda (*stopping*) The *Sailors Arms* is just down the street, on the right.

Connie Why should I want to know that?
Linda Thought you'd like to know, that's all.

Linda exits into the café

Connie wipes her hands on a cloth, removes her apron, knocks on the living-room door and enters

Connie My handbag, if you don't mind. (*She picks up her handbag*) I trust
I've not interrupted anything special. Not broken a magic spell of any sort,
I hope.

Connie exits into the street

There is a pause

Win (*vaguely and almost to herself*) I sold all your clothes.

They continue staring straight ahead

Not when you left me. (*Short pause*) Not immediately, that is. (*Pause*) I
waited a year. (*Short pause*) Well, it was nearly a year. I kept them. (*Short
pause*) In case you came back.

Bill gives a single quiet cough

I sold them. (*Pause*) The milkman had your trilby hat (*short pause*) and
your shoes, both pairs — black and brown.
Bill Oh.
Win There was no point — in keeping them.
Bill No.
Win (*after a pause*) Where did you go — when you left ... left me?
Bill (*equally vaguely*) Manchester.
Win Oh.
Bill On the train.
Win (*after a short pause*) Manchester.
Bill From Euston.
Win Yes, it would be Euston.
Bill (*after a short pause*) I cried.
Win Um?
Bill On the train.
Win Did you?
Bill In the toilet.

Win Why?
Bill A man can't cry on a train in public.
Win No. (*Short pause*) I meant — why did you cry?
Bill (*after a short pause*) I cried for a week — on and off.
Win (*after a short pause*) So did I. Longer than a week.
Bill I'm sorry.

They continue to avoid each other's eyes

Win (*after a pause*) Why Manchester?
Bill That's where the train was going.
Win I thought we were happy, but you couldn't have been — happy, that is.

There is a pause

> *Linda enters the kitchen from the café, takes a bill from the board and returns to the café*

Bill So you married again.
Win Yes. (*Pause*) Mr White. He was a bus driver. He died.
Bill I'm sorry.
Win Oh the number forty-three route.
Bill Oh.
Win Ten years ago.
Bill (*after a pause*) No children?
Win I couldn't have any children. Remember?
Bill None for me either. (*Short pause*) I never liked children——remember?
Win But you married again.
Bill (*coming in quickly*) In Australia, yes. Not here.
Win She died?
Bill Yes. After that I moved from Sydney to Douglas.
Win Who?
Bill Not who — where. Sydney Australia to Douglas ——
Win⎫ (*together*) — in the Isle of Man.
Bill⎭
Win Connie had a child. A little girl. Linda's mother, Maureen. (*Short pause*) It was George's child.
Bill Sam's child?
Win Yes, She had it before she married Dermot. Now don't say that I told you.
Bill No ... no ...
Win Connie would deny it, of course, but George is Linda's grandfather.

Bill does not react

She told me he didn't know about the baby, but I believe he did, and that's
why he left her. He never could take responsibility, that one. (*Pause*) I went
out with George a few times.
Bill You and Sam? Went out? After we were married?
Win Just a few times. To the pictures, once or twice — for a drink a few times.
Bill You didn't tell me.
Win No. You had your amateur theatricals, dancing: things like that.

*There is a pause, then the conversation continues. It starts calmly, but gathers
some pace and tension*

*Linda enters from the café during the following exchange and is attracted
by the sound of raised voices*

Bill How many times?
Win Times?
Bill Did you go out with Sam?
Win (*after a hesitation*) I don't remember.
Bill More than twice?
Win I think so.
Bill More than six times?
Win I can't remember.
Bill You must remember.
Win Does it matter now?
Bill More than six?
Win Maybe. Maybe more than six. It's so long ago.
Bill It does matter.
Win (*standing up*) Nothing can matter that happened that long ago.
Bill I say it does.
Win I say it doesn't. (*Short pause*) It was more. More than six — nearer
twelve times. Maybe more than twelve. How can it possibly matter now,
at our age, after all this time?
Bill (*standing up*) It does matter to me.
Win (*picking up her handbag*) You're being silly. (*She moves towards the
street door*) I never did like you when you were being silly. (*She becomes
distressed*) I'm sorry, Arthur.

Win exits through the street door

Bill (*pensively*) It matters to me now, Winifred, because had I known then
… (*He sits at the table*)

Connie enters the kitchen from the café

Linda Oh! Have you found him?
Connie Who?
Linda Sam — George.
Connie Yes, I have.
Linda Thought you would.
Connie Are those two still in there?
Linda Yes, I think so. I heard raised voices just now. What happened in the *Sailors Arms*? Did you continue the aggro with bad Sam?
Connie There was no aggro. He'll be back soon.
Linda When you've gone. He won't be back before then.
Connie You're wrong, Miss Know-all. You're wrong. (*She moves to the living-room door*) It's very quiet in there now.
Linda I heard them — just a minute ago. (*Lightly*) Perhaps Winnie has knifed him.

Connie knocks on the door and slowly opens it

Connie Oh! You're on your own.
Bill (*nervously*) Yes.
Connie Where's Winnie?
Bill (*standing up*) She's gone out.
Connie Where to?
Bill I don't know.
Connie (*returning to Linda*) Can you cope all right in here?
Linda What d'you think I've been doing here since whenever? Playing Ludo? (*She starts washing up during the following*)
Connie (*closing the door; with some vehemence but with lowered voice*) Well — now — then — Arthur Wilkins. What the hell happened to you forty years ago?
Bill Me? D'you mean — me going away?
Connie Of course that's what I mean. You going away and leaving me.
Bill No, I didn't leave you. I left Winifred, George left you.
Connie I could accept George going. Always on the cards, that one, but not you. We had something a bit special, I thought, you and me.
Bill Did we?
Connie Did we? You know we did.
Bill (*after a hesitation*) Yes, but it was getting ... well ... getting complicated.
Connie You can't hare off like a rabbit when things get complicated.
Bill That's all there was for me to do. George going away left me with you and Winifred. I couldn't face up to that dilemma. I couldn't face up to choosing. And I wanted to get back to the stage.
Connie George, at least, left a scrappy note. You didn't have the decency to do that.

Bill There was nowhere I could leave a note.

Connie Well, then, you could have said something, even if it was just "Cheerio."

Bill You would have made a fuss. I didn't think it was important.

Connie Important? Blimey, it was important to me. I was carrying your child.

Bill What?

Connie You heard.

Bill No, you were not.

Connie Oh, yes I was. That girl in there is your flesh and blood, Arthur. Her mother was your child. There's no getting away from that.

Bill It was George's child.

Connie Oh, no. I said it was George's child. Now that's a different thing altogether. Fortunately, I married again; Dermot took us both in. A drinker he may have been, but Dermot had character.

Bill stands and moves to the window

Sam enters the kitchen from the café

Sam (*lightly*) Remember me? I used to work here.

Linda So there you are.

Sam Yes, here I am.

Connie (*to Bill*) I thought I'd tell you — about Linda, that's all.

Bill I never liked children.

Linda (*to Sam*) You sound cheerful. Didn't think you'd be back yet.

Sam What are you doing?

Linda What d'you think I'm doing? Picking my nose?

Connie (*to Bill*) You wouldn't have liked your daughter, Linda's mother. I called her Maureen. She turned out to be no good.

Sam (*to Linda*) Where is everybody?

Linda They're in there.

Sam moves to the living-room door

Connie (*to Bill*) I haven't set eyes on our Maureen for ... it must be fourteen years. Her husband left her. I brought Linda up on my own — well, with Dermot.

Linda (*to Sam*) What did our Nan say to you? Did you kiss and make up?

Sam Not quite.

Connie (*to Bill*) It seems I've lived all my life with wayward kids and no good men.

Linda (*to Sam*) Fancy you and our Nan having it away together.

Sam We were married.

Bill (*to Connie.*) I can't say I like the girl — what I've seen of her.
Connie Linda? (*She considers*)
Linda (*to Sam*) I can't believe any of what's happening here … .
Connie (*to Bill*) Linda's all right — sometimes.
Linda (*to Sam*) It's like a rotten film.
Sam A tragedy?
Linda A comedy, more like. 'Ere, you and me is nearly related.
Sam But we're not.
Linda It was close.
Sam Very close.
Connie (*to Bill*) You could get to like Linda.
Bill No, I don't think I could — I'm sorry.
Sam (*moving to the living-room door*) It's very quiet in there.
Linda Something funky about that room today. They all go weird in there.
Sam (*opening the living-room door and entering*) Hallo! Is this a private club or can anyone join?

Linda exits into the café

There is a short pause

Where's Winifred?
Connie She's out.
Sam Oh?
Bill (*standing*) Will you excuse me, please.

Bill crosses the living-room and hurries up the stairs

Sam What's the matter with Bill?
Connie I've no idea.
Sam (*calling up the stairs*) Bill? (*To Connie, lightly*) Now, have you been upsetting him?
Connie No. And his name is Arthur. (*Short pause*) So, you decided to come back.
Sam I didn't decide. You asked me to.
Connie Well, it was stupid, running off like that. Is running away your answer to everything?
Sam Most times, yes, I think it is.
Connie Not much of a life, George. You might say that. But you never married again.
Sam Never in one place long enough. Facing up to things isn't necessarily a virtue. It is possible to live by facing up to very little. A person who keeps constantly on the move, offends other people less and pleases himself more.

Connie You've been lucky getting away with that, George. I've faced up to my responsibilities. It's been no joke for me, not when I look back.

Sam Ah, but never look back, Connie, never do that. You must look to the future.

Connie Future! Hah! Not together.

Sam I didn't say together. It never worked the first time round, did it. We were too young: growing up together, as kids, then straight into marriage.

Connie I was nineteen.

Sam We were children. Anyway, I'm sure you don't need me.

Connie I didn't say I needed you, did I? Heaven forbid! (*After a pause; defensively*) Don't think I'm lonely. I have the customers in the pub. They're a good crowd. Anyway, I'd hate to have somebody like you about the place again.

Sam And I'm sure you're right.

Connie (*after a pause; pensively*) Yet there are times when it would be nice to have someone, when the pub is shut and it's quiet. A face perhaps, just to talk to. A pub is very silent when it's shut.

Linda enters the kitchen from the café and moves into the living-room

Linda (*to Connie*) Your friend, Win, is in the café now. She's ordered an orange juice.

Connie (*recovering*) What's she doing in there, for heaven's sake? Silly woman. (*She moves into the kitchen*) What's she up to?

Connie exits into the café

Linda (*to Sam*) Are you all right, then? Sam?

Sam Yes, I'm all right. Why don't you shut this place for the rest of the day?

Linda No! I'm enjoying it. For the first time in my life I feel important — and I'm needed. Don't spoil it.

Sam Shouldn't you be replacing Hemel Hempstead at this time?

Linda (*evasively*) I have work to do here, don't I? Where's Bill?

Sam He's up there. I'm not sure why. (*He moves to the bottom of the stairs*) I'll see.

Linda I'll get the orange juice. (*She moves into the kitchen and pours a glass of orange juice during the following*)

Sam (*calling*) Bill? What are you doing up there?

Sam climbs the stairs and exits

Connie enters the kitchen from the café. She is towing a reluctant Win

Connie What d'you think you're doing, Winifred, leaving me in there?

Win (*sharply*) I don't wish to be involved any more, thank you.
Connie Then why creep back into the café like that?
Win I was waiting for you.

Bill descends the stairs into the living-room, carrying a suitcase. Sam follows

Connie People who creep about annoy me. When we leave here, which will be very soon, we'll do so in a dignified manner, not scuttling off like two little dogs. Talking of which, where are George and Arthur? (*She leads Win to the living-room door*)
Linda (*holding out the glass of orange juice*) One orange juice? Winnie?

Connie, leading Win, ignores Linda and moves into the living-room. Linda shrugs her shoulders, places the glass down and continues working

Connie So there you are.
Sam (*falsely cheerful*) That's right, here we are. (*His attention is attracted by Bill's suitcase*) What's the next move? Whose throw is it now?
Connie It's not a game, George. We've come to say we're going now. Leaving the two of you in peace.
Sam Oh, I see. (*He glances at Bill*)

Bill does not react

Connie That will please most people, I'm sure. What are you doing with that case, Arthur?
Bill I'm leaving.
Connie Leaving here? What d'you mean? Leaving for good?
Bill Yes, I think so.
Connie Why are you doing that? We're going now.
Sam He won't stay. He's made up his mind.
Bill It doesn't matter.
Win (*to Bill*) It does matter.
Bill I've never really felt comfortable here — in a café. It's not my kind of thing.
Sam That's not true.
Win (*winding herself up*) No! I'll tell you why he's leaving. It's because I've told him something.
Connie Oh?
Win I told him something that happened too long ago to matter.
Bill No, it's not that.
Connie (*sardonically*) And what important revelation would that have been then, Winifred?

Win (*innocently*) I told him that I went out with George ... a few times.

Connie You went out with George? What d'you mean exactly? You went out with George when he was married to me?

Win Yes.

Connie You had some kind of affair with my George?

Win I'm not sure that I know what an affair is. We went out together a few times, that's all.

Connie That's all? Going out with my husband behind my back.

Win Connie, it was all so long ago.

Connie You crafty little bitch! George, what have you to say about that?

Sam Me? I hardly remember.

Connie Well, no, of course you wouldn't. A convenient loss of memory. Well then, Winifred, I don't want to spoil your little moment of glory, but I suspect that Arthur is running away because of another completely different reason and nothing to do with you. I'm sorry! You see, your husband, Arthur, and me *were* having an affair. Yes — and I do know what that word means.

Win No!

Connie And we were doing just that.

Bill Connie, please ...

Sam What? You and — and him? You and Bill?

Connie Arthur ——

Sam (*to Bill*) Now, Bill that can't be right.

Bill does not react

I don't believe it.

Connie Why should you care? You never cared about me then.

Sam I didn't know then, did I.

Connie Well, you know now.

Sam Old Bill wouldn't have the guts.

Connie Neither of you had any guts. Dermot had more than the pair of you put together.

The following exchange, although building in tension, is not bitter or vindictive. It is childlike and almost comical

Sam And he would have needed it with you.

Win (*to Connie, bursting*) Why don't you tell him the whole truth? Why don't you tell George that Linda is his own flesh and blood?

Connie Shut your mouth, Winnie!

Sam (*puzzled*) Lewisham is nothing to do with me.

Win Yes she is. She had the baby before she married Dermot. She told me it was yours.

Connie Winifred, shut up!

Win No! I've kept quiet all these years, because you asked me to. But Dermot has passed on, so it doesn't matter. (*To Sam*) She's your granddaughter, Linda is.

Linda slowly enters the living-room during the following lines, which gather pace and merge

Connie Winnie, will you please shut your mouth.
Sam Is that right?
Win It's the truth.

Connie takes hold of Win

Connie It's not the truth! You know it's not the truth …
Win Stop it! Stop it! Let go of me …

Bill parts Win from Connie and remains holding on to Win

Bill Now, now! It doesn't matter now …
Connie (*to Win*) You've gone too far. Too far this time.

Sam moves in to extricate Bill from Win. The general grappling and noise is almost comical; they are like four small children

Sam Come on, take your hands off her.

Sam and Win move away from Bill. Connie moves forward

(*To Connie*) And you keep away.
Win I'm telling the truth. What about you and Arthur?
Connie She's a liar!
Bill (*to Sam*) Keep your hands off her.

Sam lets go of Win and he and Bill become locked together. Connie and Win try to part them

Linda closes the kitchen door and stands on a chair

Linda Will you all shut up! Shut up for God's sake! (*Silence*) You're like four little kids, all of you — like kids. (*She steps down from the chair*) Now, why don't you all sit down? All sit down.

The others hesitate

Go on! Go on! Sit down.

Linda ushers the others to the chairs around the table

Sit — sit — sit.

Connie Who d'you think you're ordering about?

Linda You! All of you. You're worse than kids, you are. Now, I haven't much time; I have my customers waiting. Right? Now, I reckon, before you break your silly heads and have heart attacks, you should take a check on yourselves. You're pathetic, that's what you are. You make a cock-up of things years ago and now you're doing it all again. Looks to me, you screwed it up at the start. You married the wrong one.

Connie What are you talking about?

Linda Now listen! Right? You two, Sam and Nan, are OK people but all mouth — rabbit, rabbit, jaw, jaw. The same sort, always looking to score on each other. No chance! (*She turns to Bill and Win*) Now you two, Bill and Win, are nice people but mouse, mouse, softly, softly boring — never scoring at all. No chance either. (*She points at Connie*) Now: if you'd married Bill and (*she points at Win*) you'd married Sam, you may have got it right at the start. Right? But here you are, getting old, and none of you got anybody. So why not give it a go with the other one? You could finish off your days with a little bit of whatever you get up to at your sort of age.

The phone rings

Think about it. I'll get that. (*She crosses to the phone and lifts the receiver*)

The quartet at the table sit in glazed thought

(*Into the phone*) Hallo? ... This is Linda ... Yes, I know who that is. It's Vince ... What d'you want? ... Really! ... Well, thanks for asking me, but I've had enough of you, Vince ... That's right! ... I'm busy running a café ... No, I'm not being funny ... And the same to you, Vince! But I don't need you — goodbye. (*She slams the receiver down*) Now, you four, I have work to do. Behave yourselves. (*She turns to Sam; with some tenderness*) Sam. I'm pleased you're my granddad — I'm very pleased about that.

Linda moves into the kitchen and then exits into the café

Connie, Sam, Bill and Win remain at the table with fixed expressions

Connie (*deliberately*) She really has too much mouth, that girl.

Sam Out of the mouths of babes ... .

Connie Comes forth a lot of bleedin' nonsense most of the time.
Sam (*after a short pause*) When all is said and done we're not the same people as forty years ago.
Bill Too true.
Win Time changes all things. So they say.
Connie Is it too late for us to change?
Sam It's never too late to change — some things.

Bill stands up and moves nervously towards his case

Connie Are you still going, Arthur?
Bill Yes, I am.
Connie (*standing*) Where?
Bill I don't know. I'm not sure.
Connie Have you thought about London?
Bill Not often.
Connie Then you should. Lewisham's a decent sort of place.
Bill I'm sure it is.
Connie If you close your eyes and think of somewhere else.
Bill If you say so.
Connie I do say so. I'm going to get myself a lunch in a proper café. Will you be joining me?
Bill Me?
Connie Yes. Who else is there? I'll be catching the train to London this evening.
Bill I see. (*He picks up his case*) Well, it's my move — I think. (*He heads towards the street door*)
Sam (*standing up*) Bill?

Bill stops

What about the Ludo game? Shall I keep it in the hold position?
Bill It's up to you.
Sam I might as well. Just in case. For as long as the Blutack holds?
Bill (*with a faint smile*) Yes — why not.

Bill turns and exits into the street leaving the door ajar

Connie What about you, Winifred? What are you going to do?
Sam She'll be staying here.
Win I haven't said that … .
Sam For lunch? You'll be staying here for a proper lunch.
Win Well, I don't know … .

Sam You'll be quite all right with me.

Win Will I?

Sam Of course you will.

Win (*after a short pause*) If you say so.

Connie (*to Win*) Please yourself, dear. Please yourself. I shall certainly be leaving here now. And later on I'll be catching the six-thirty train, if you're interested, Winifred. I must be in the pub tomorrow, that's for sure.

Sam And Linda?

Connie What about her? Now that I know Linda can please herself. She has to leave the nest at some time. If it's not this week then it will be next, so it makes no difference to me now. (*Short pause*) George, I'd like to say it's been nice seeing you again but … (*She considers*) Well, I suppose it has — in a way. Pleased to see you keeping so well.

Sam You too, Connie.

Connie At least we know where we are now, if you know what I mean.

Sam Yes, we know where we are.

Connie (*after a short pause*) Well, I'll say cheerio then.

Sam Yes. Cheerio then.

Connie exits into the street

Sam closes the front door, then turns to Win at the table. There is a pause

Hallo.

Win (*not turning*) Hallo.

Sam How strange it is …

Win Um?

Sam Meeting again like this.

Win It is strange. I would have passed you in the street.

Sam And I wouldn't have recognized you either.

Win (*after a short pause*) What will happen to Arthur?

Sam He may be the face that Connie can talk to — when the pub is silent.

Win What d'you mean?

Sam Do you live alone?

Win Yes.

Sam Loneliness is not a good thing.

Win It's all right. Being alone doesn't mean you have to be unhappy. I'm quite happy, most of the time. I go to bingo — and there's Mr Wainwright. (*Pause*) My chiropodist. I do enjoy having my feet done. He's a very nice man. Very gentle.

Sam That's good.

Win (*pause*) And what will you be doing now?

Sam Me? I think perhaps it's time I was moving on. I've been here for more than two years. I've rarely stayed anywhere for that length of time.

Win You can't keep running away, George.

Sam I can, if I have to.

Win You have to stop at some time. D'you know what my mother used to say? She used to say: "There comes a time when you must stop, put the pig on the wall, and watch the band go by."

Sam And I must be in the band. I can't be still and do nothing.

Win There's nowhere for me to run, I'm pleased to say.

Sam (*after a pause*) I don't suppose, by any chance, you would consider staying here with me?

Win George, what a question …

Sam Just for a few days …

Linda enters the kitchen from the café with an order

Linda (*shouting cheerfully*) Four ham rolls, two coffees — table two. (*She stabs the order on hook two*) And two people on table one are from Japan. Will you be confirming that one?

Sam Right, young lady! I'll be with you. (*He moves towards the door to the kitchen*) Winifred, you'll stay for lunch? (*He enters the kitchen*)

Linda (*to Sam*) Look at it all in here. Didn't I tell you, you needed a pair of young legs?

Sam You did, you did, but don't knock old legs ——

Linda⎫
Sam ⎭ (*together*) They can knock on their own.

Win stands, cautiously moves towards the street door and exits during the following

Linda Look, there's the order for table two, and there's washing up to be done. I have to clear up the tables in the café … (*She stops*)

Sam ⎫
Linda⎭ (*together*) It's not a café!

Linda exits into the café

Sam sets to work in the kitchen

Sam (*at length*) Winifred, are you skilled in the trades of washing and wiping up? (*He continues working*) Did you hear what I said? (*He reacts to the silence by moving to the living-room door and looking through it*) Winifred? (*He sees the open street door, crosses slowly to it and hesitates before closing it. He pauses, then moves to the table, picks up the dice cup,* *shakes it and throws the dice)* Five. (*He moves slowly to the dining table and sits*

After a pause the street door opens . Bill enters tentatively, carrying his case

Bill Hallo.

Sam turns

D'you have room for a pair of old legs?
Sam (*standing*) Indeed I do.
Bill Don't knock old legs.
Sam Never do that.

There is a pause. They hold a look

(*Warmly*) I had a feeling you'd be back.
Bill I thought you might. I've been waiting in Sid's fishing tackle shop.
Sam That's a useful little shop, Sid's, for waiting and watching.
Bill It is. I saw them go — Connie and Winifred. There's really no point in living in times past, I thought.
Sam And you thought right. And we mustn't forget our pastimes. I do believe it's your turn on the Ludo. (*He hands Bill the cup*)
Bill (*with a sparkle*) Yes. Yes, I believe you're right. (*He puts his case down and moves to the Ludo board*) You realize I'm winning?
Sam Don't get over-confident. It's first past the post who wins.
Bill (*shaking the dice*) Watch now — watch. (*He rolls the dice*) Five!
Sam Not a bad throw, granted.
Bill Things are looking better already.
Sam (*taking the cup and dice*) They could be. (*He shakes the dice*) The way the dice falls dictates the game. (*He continues shaking the dice*) We shall see.

The Lights fade. All we hear is the sound of the rattling dice as Sam prolongs his throw

CURTAIN

FURNITURE AND PROPERTY LIST

ACT I
SCENE 1

On stage: KITCHEN

Kitchen units with work surfaces. *On units*: kettle, coffee, tea, orange squash, **Sam**'s notebook, trays, spare pencils. *In units*: cutlery, cheese biscuits, table-cloth, Bran Flakes, pastries, dustpan and brush, sugar jar, bottle of vinegar, bread, pickled onions

Shelves. *On them*: crockery, pans etc. *On one*: small tape recorder

Stainless steel sink with drainer and practical taps. *On it*: washing up liquid, washing-up cloth, used crockery and cutlery. *Nearby*: teacloths

Small hand washbasin

Cooker (not practical)

Microwave oven. *In it*: six jacket potatoes

Cool chest

Refrigerator. *In it*: blackcurrant cheesecake, cheese on cheeseboard, jug of milk, tuna flan, apple pie, jug of cream, quiche, Scotch eggs, orange juice, ham

Freezer. *In it*: ice-cream

Small varnished board with seven numbered hooks. Orders on hooks one, two, three, four and six

LIVING-ROOM

Beneath staircase: carpet-sweeper

Small dining table

Four small chairs

Small armchair

Large drinks cabinet or sideboard. *In a drawer*: boxed game of tiddly-winks. *In cabinet*: bottle of whisky, glass

Small table. *On it*: unfinished game of Ludo with dice and shaker

Small table. *On it*: telephone

Wall shelving. *On it*: paperback books

Off stage: Order (**Sam**)

Order (**Bill**)

Holdall bag (**Linda**)

Personal: **Sam**: pen, wristwatch (worn throughout)

SCENE 2

Set: Sleeping bag for **Linda**

Strike: Remove all orders from order board

SCENE 3

Set: Salad items in containers (tomatoes, coleslaw, parsley, onion, cucumber, lettuce)

Re-set: Stick Ludo counters down with Blutack

Off stage: Tray and order (**Sam**)

Personal: **Connie**: handbag
                    Winnie: handbag

ACT II

SCENE 1

Set: Orders on hooks three and five

Off stage: Tray holding two empty sugar pots, items of crockery; order (**Linda**)
                    Order and bill (**Linda**)
                    Tray of used cutlery and crockery (**Linda**)
                    Empty vinegar bottle (**Linda**)
                    Tray and order (**Linda**)
                    Order (**Bill**)

Personal: **Linda**: order

SCENE 2

Set: Order on hook one (Remove all others)

Off stage: Suitcase (**Bill**)
                    Order (**Linda**)

LIGHTING PLOT

Practical fittings needed: nil

Interior with exterior window backing. The same scene throughout

ACT I, Scene 1

To open: General interior lighting with late evening effect on exterior backing

No cues

ACT I, Scene 2

To open: Dim interior lighting with bright sun effect on exterior backing

Cue 1   **Linda** opens the curtains   (Page 10)
             Bring up interior lighting

ACT I, Scene 3

To open: General interior lighting with bright sun effect on exterior backing

No cues

ACT II, Scene 1

To open: Same lighting state as ACT I, Scene 3

No cues

ACT II, Scene 2

To open: Same lighting state as ACT II, Scene 1

Cue 2   **Sam**: "We shall see."   (Page 74)
             The lights fade

EFFECTS PLOT

ACT I

Cue 1   As ACT I, SCENE 3 begins   (Page 25)
             Microwave timer pings

ACT II

Cue 2   **Linda** exits into the café   (Page 45)
             Microwave timer pings

Cue 3   **Linda**: " ... at your sort of age."   (Page 70)
             Phone rings